Ko Family

ALL
GOD'S
CREATURES

ALL GOD'S CREATURES

Inspirational Stories About the Animals That We Love

Compiled by the Editors of Guideposts

This edition published in 1996 by SMITHMARK Publishers, a division of US Media Holdings, Inc., 16 East 32nd Street, New York, NY 10016.

SMITHMARK books are available for bulk purchase for sales, promotion, and premium use. For details, write or call the manager of special sales, SMITHMARK Publishers, 16 East 32nd Street, New York, NY 10016 (212) 532-6600.

Except as noted on page 172, all material originally appeared in *Guideposts* magazine, or in *Daily Guideposts*. Copyright © 1950, 1958, 1959, 1966, 1970, 1971, 1973, 1976, 1983, 1984, 1985, 1986, 1987, 1988, 1989, 1990, 1991, 1992, 1993.

All God's creatures / compiled by the editors of Guideposts
      p.   cm.
    Originally published: Carmel, N.Y. (39 Seminary Hill Road, Carmel 10512): Guideposts Associates, © 1993.
    Includes bibliographical references.
    ISBN 0-8317-7502-5
    1. Animals—Religious aspects—Christianity—Anecdotes I. Guideposts (Pawling, N.Y.)
[BT746.A45   1996]
242-dc20   95-46992
                                                                             CIP

Printed in the USA

10 9 8 7 6 5 4 3 2 1

CONTENTS

PREFACE

*I*t's a little story I often tell. I'd left the office and was walking through Central Park at the time of day when New Yorkers come home and their dogs come out. The scene was all too familiar, and I was a bit wistful, for this was the part of the park where I used to run my pointer Clay before he died at the ripe dog-age of thirteen. I watched the usual incongruous collection of canines sniffing and yelping and chasing one another, and there stood the usual incongruous collection of people, chatting as ever on the subject that had drawn them together, their animals. Suddenly a woman came up to me with a happy look of recognition on her face. "Hello, there," she said. "I remember you. You're Clay's father!"

That's the way it is with pet people. After a while the distinctions they make between biped and quadruped tend to blur. And that, it seems to me, is not at all unreasonable. Pet people are inclined to recognize a fact that non-pet people often fail to see, that we are all animals, that God created the creeping thing even before the human being, that both are fellow creatures upon which He looks with favor.

The stories in this book are chiefly about our pets, but you cannot read them without concluding that what we think of as lesser animals, wild or domesticated, are all part of the grand design. We need them as they need us, and they give to us, as we give to them. I thought of this recently when a friend started taking his young yellow Labrador retriever to obedience classes. I couldn't help but smile as Edward told me of his dog Marty's progress. I wondered if he realized that his dog was not the only student in school. Marty was learning to sit and heel, but Edward was learning to be patient and responsible and how to convey his love wisely. He was learning to cohabitate, which is an obedience we all need to be schooled in.

So read these stories for the pleasure they will provide, but be prepared for what they have to say about caring, about give and take, about living together. They are not just about the animals of the field and air and stream, they are about you and me too, for we are all creatures of God, His instruments.

——*Van Varner*
Editorial Director

Introduction

God and the Animals

GOD BLESS OUR ANIMALS

Van Varner

$\mathcal{E}$very year on the first Sunday in May in the gardens of the Hammond Museum in North Salem, New York, a group of interfaith clergy perform a "Blessing of the Animals." The custom is an ancient one, now observed chiefly in European churches, but it was new to me and I drove up for it.

I'm glad I did. It was something to see. Men, women and children formed a long line, their pets in hand or in tow: dogs and cats, ponies and horses, birds, turtles, goldfish, ferrets, etc., etc., etc. One little boy even brought his terrarium. (I did not ask what about-to-be-blessed animals lurked inside the greenery!)

It was a lovely ritual. My face must have looked like one big benign smile as I watched these dumb creatures presenting muzzle, beak and fin for the Lord's benediction. What I did not expect, however, among the mingling of the animals was their calm demeanor—not a yap or yowl or chirp from any in that long, decorous parade. It was a peaceable kingdom . . .

Except . . .

. . . for Renée. A peach-colored poodle, she was not in the procession. She had come with her master, a handicapped man from New Jersey who was confined to a wheelchair. Renée sat beside him in the audience and barked and howled at every animal that passed by.

"Dumb creatures," did I say? From biped to centipede, which one of us wants to be left out of the Lord's blessing?

I'd bark, too, Renée.

GOD'S PLAN

Marilyn Morgan Helleberg

I wasn't ready for my daughter's question. We were walking through greening prairie grass along the edge of the Platte River south of Kearney, where we had camped to watch the annual sandhill crane extravaganza. It was the second week in April and about time for the birds to leave the area for their breeding grounds in the northlands.

Every year in early March, it seems as if the sky opens up and rains birds. Some five hundred thousand cranes spread out over the cornfields of mid-Nebraska, preening themselves, feeding, prancing around in a dance of life that is centuries old yet always fresh and new. For about six weeks they leap and soar and cry at the wind, bringing the grace and the splendor and the pain of poetry into our lives. Then they're gone again, leaving an emptiness on the prairies and in our lives that's a kind of poetry, too.

Maybe it was the thought of those birds and their invisibly guided journey that made Karen ask, with a thirteen-year-old's trust in absolutes, "How can I find out God's purpose for my life, Mom?"

I searched for an answer as we stood on the river bank, listening to the sound of the flowing waters punctuated by the wild, echoing calls of the cranes. But no solid answer came. For the rest of the afternoon, we continued to watch and listen. Then about 4:30, as the April day began to pull down its shades and the bridge cast long-fingered shadows onto the river, we gathered up our camping gear and walked back to the car. There seemed to be an urgency in the flock now. The playful dance of the birds gave way to a nervous pecking at grain, a noisy chattering, a restless flapping of wings. We sat quietly in the car for a while, watching the drama, knowing that an ancient ritual was about to be enacted.

Suddenly, as if gathered into oneness by some great unseen force, a whole field full of birds lifted into the air. For several moments, the sky was a chaos of flapping wings, straining legs, and stretching necks. Then, in obedience to some internal sense of unity, ragged lines and clusters began to merge. The formation became a single, immense body darkening the sky, circling around and around and around, and finally sweeping across the horizon with measured wing beat, heading northward. A few more minutes and that wide Nebraska sky was clear except for a few pink-tinged clouds . . . and the afterglow of wonder that comes from the incredible grace of seeing with new eyes.

I wasn't able to give Karen a pat answer to her question about the purpose of her life. Perhaps each of us has to answer (and re-answer) that question for ourselves. Yet as we talked quietly throughout the afternoon, I think I was able to pass on to her my solid conviction that God most certainly does have a plan for each life. There was something about the mystery and the splendor of those cranes that seemed to confirm that belief. Watching them was like seeing a parable enacted. It helped us to know that even those events that seem to be random are part of a greater and intensely purposeful wholeness. God's hand, although invisible, is reliable and can be trusted. Just as the cranes find their way, not by trying to control their situation but by flowing with invisible forces, so we can find our way through life by relinquishing each incident, each moment, each relationship . . . everything in our lives to God.

ON THE TOP OF THE WORLD

John H. Blue

I was nineteen years old and just out of school when I packed a sledge one day, preparatory to making a trip some five hundred miles north of Dawson, up in the Yukon. This was to be the first Christmas I had ever spent alone, and my most hazardous journey in the dead of winter.

My objective was to chart a ledge that was only partly indicated on a crude map drawn two years previously. The markings on the map were reliable, but I hardly anticipated the variety of hazards ahead.

The trail was over ice and snow, frozen rivers and lakes, and steep grades and rock hills. I knew I could expect blizzards, hungry wild life and always the peril of food shortage if delayed for any length of time.

I have never started on a trip of this type without talking straight to God, making it clear what my mission is and asking His divine protection for both myself and my dogs. I believe His help can come while I'm "on the run," or when in a church, if the prayer is honest and sincere.

On December 24, 1908, I was camped about two hundred and fifty miles out of Dawson, in a desolate moonlit spot, with nothing but snow-covered mountains in the distance, and the dogs by my side.

The weather had been fine, and the going good, all of which made me deeply grateful. While preparing my Christmas Eve meal of tea and bacon over the pitch stick fire, I thought of my family, thousands of miles away, around the fireplace and Christmas gifts under the tree.

I could see the faces and guessed much of the talk that was going on. I also knew that Mother was thinking just as strongly about me and my progress as I was of her and the rest of the family. It seemed as if I could hear her prayer. I straightened up and said, "God, You are being good to me and my dogs. I know You will comfort Mother in her thoughts, and let her know that I am all right, and not lonely or cold, even though far away."

I was startled from my thoughts by a hissing sound in the distance. In seconds, the hisses changed to sharp, crackling reports. I looked around quickly as the sounds grew louder. I saw the sky begin to brighten in the north. Multicolored shafts of light shot skyward. The glory of it took my breath away! It was the aurora borealis in full splendor.

There I was with a reserved seat at a private showing of the greatest Christmas pageant one can ever hope to see. All the colors of the rainbow reflected on the snow-covered mountains and flickered over the smooth, snowy surface. It had the effect of a magnificent, shimmering oriental rug.

Just then, the dogs began to growl. They were tense. They stood still as iron statues. I scanned the horizon. There, coming towards us from the distance, was a pack of wolves. All the beauty was suddenly blacked out in the thought of self-preservation.

I knew my dogs and I were windward from the pack. I hoped the brilliant lights would distract them from seeing us too easily.

But for how long?

To my dismay the wolves formed a large circle about a hundred yards in front of us. I could count fourteen wolves. Then the leader of the pack took his place in the center of that sitting circle and began to howl to the moon. Soon, there was a full chorus of fourteen howling, hardly symphonic voices.

For over an hour this howling kept up as my tension mounted. Then, as the aurora borealis began to sink back into the northern earth, the leader of the pack abruptly stopped his howling, turned, and started back in the direction from which he had come. The others filed behind him.

I was relieved, puzzled, and so in awe I could hardly believe what I had seen. Had the wolves put on a worship ceremony for my benefit? I've never heard a church bell ring since but that I don't recall this, my most spectacular Christmas experience.

Part One

LEARNING
FROM
GOD'S
CREATURES

I

Friendship

The Swan and the Goose

Charlotte Edwards

$\mathcal{W}$ here we live, on the Eastern Shore of Maryland, the gentle waters run in and out like fingers slimming at the tips. They curl into the smaller creeks and coves like tender palms.

The Canada geese know this, as do the fat white swans and the ducks who ride an inch above the waves of Chesapeake Bay as they skim their way into harbor. In the autumn, by the thousands, they come home for the winter.

In hunting season the air is filled with the sound of guns. The shores are scattered with blinds, the creeks and rivers with duck and goose decoys. The swans are a different matter entirely. Protected by law, they move toward the shores in a stately glide, their tall heads proud and unafraid. They lower their long necks deep into the water, where their strong beaks dig through the river bottoms for food.

And there is between the arrogant swans and the prolific geese an indifference, almost a disdain.

Once or twice each year, snow and sleet move into the area. When this happens, if the river is at its narrowest, or the creek shallow, there is a freeze that hardens the water to ice.

It was on such a morning near Oxford, Maryland, that a friend of mine set the breakfast table and poured the coffee beside the huge window that looked out from her home on the Tred Avon River. Across the river, beyond the dock, the snow laced the rim of the shore in white. For a moment she stood quietly, looking at what the night's storm had painted.

Suddenly she leaned forward and peered close to the frosted window. "It really is," she cried aloud. "There's a goose out there."

She reached to the bookcase and pulled out a pair of binoculars. Into their sights came the figure of a large Canada goose, very still, its wings folded tight to its sides, its feet frozen to the ice.

Then from the dark sky, white against its lackluster, she saw a line of swans. They moved in their own singular formation, graceful, intrepid and free. They crossed from the west of the broad creek high above the house, moving steadily to the east.

As my friend watched, the leader swung to the right. Then the white string of birds became a white circle. It floated from the top of the sky downward. At last, as easy as feathers coming to earth, the circle landed on the ice.

My friend was on her feet now, with one unbelieving hand against her mouth. As the swans surrounded the frozen goose, she feared that what life he still maintained might be pecked out by those great swan bills.

Instead, amazingly instead, those bills began to work on the ice. The long necks were lifted and curved down, again and again, as deliberately as picks swung over the head of a fisherman cutting a free space for his winter rod. It went on for a long time.

At last the goose was rimmed by a narrow margin of ice instead of the entire creek. The swans rose again, following the leader, and hovered in that circle, awaiting the results of their labors.

The goose's head was lifted. Its body pulled. Then the goose was free and standing on the ice. He was moving his big webbed feet slowly. And the swans stood in the air over him, watching.

Then as if he had cried, "I cannot fly," four of the swans came down around him. Their powerful beaks scraped the goose's wing from bottom to top, scuttled under its wings and rode up its body, chipping off and melting the ice held in the feathers.

Slowly, as if testing, the goose spread its wings as far as they would go, brought them together, accordionlike, and spread again.

When at last the wings reached their full, the four swans took off and joined the hovering group. They resumed their eastward journey, in perfect, impersonal formation, to a secret destination.

Behind them, rising with incredible speed and joy, the goose moved into the sky. He followed them, flapping double time, until he caught up, until he joined the last of the line, like a small dark child at the end of a crack-the-whip of older boys.

My friend watched them until they disappeared over the tips of the farthest trees. Only then, in the dusk that was suddenly deep, did she realize that tears were running down her cheeks and had been for how long she didn't know.

This is a true story. It happened. I do not try to interpret it. I just think of it in the bad moments, and from it comes only one hopeful question: "If so for birds, why not for people?"

THE WELCOMING GULLS

Marjorie Holmes

This morning the silver-gray lake is combed with long, long waves, each perfectly spaced and formed. Above the waves, white and shining in the sun, the gulls dip and soar. And riding the crests below, along with a scattering of gulls, we are surprised to see hundreds of ducks. Great flocks of these smaller, darker visitors, guarded and shepherded, it seems, by the gulls!

No, no, impossible, we must be imagining things. Yet even as we watch, more gulls are flying off as if to greet the other flocks we can see approaching, and escort them in. Yes, yes, here they come, descending together. Then, as the noisy strangers are settling down, a few gulls move about among them, getting acquainted. "Are you comfortable?" they seem to be asking. "Rest a while, do some fishing, it's very good here. Call us if you need anything."

For hours the ducks dive for fish, or rock contentedly on the long silver waves. Then, toward late afternoon, they begin to flutter upward. And a few of the gulls join their departing guests and soar with them briefly, as if to say good-bye.

How amazing! Such hospitality and generosity. We always thought wild things were selfish, treating any strangers as intruders, guarding their own feeding grounds against them, driving them away. And most of them do. Yet "our gulls," the lovely birds that soar across our lakeside cottage, so familiar they seem like family, have treated the ducks like long-lost friends!

I suggest to my husband: "That new family that's just moved in . . . let's invite them over for dinner."

LONELY FOR A FRIEND

Penney Schwab

As part of a 4-H project, my daughter Rebecca had two show steers. Howie, a lazy red, spent his days at the feed trough. Nick, sleek and black, preferred to play. While Howie got fat, Nick chased the cats who sought shelter in his shed. At the County Fair, Howie was the second-place heavy-weight, while Nick was champion lightweight. Howie went through the sale ring; Nick came back to the farm.

But the very next morning Nick was gone. After a two-hour search we found him in the stubble field with a bunch of feeder steer. Rebecca put an extra wire on the gate, but less than a week later Nick disappeared again. This time we found him six miles from home, grazing contentedly beside an old white cow.

Driving home, Rebecca said, "Mom, I think I know what's wrong. Nick is lonely. He needs a friend." It sounded silly, but as soon as Nick was in his pen, we took the trailer to the corral and picked a scrubby steer to be Nick's companion. Nick never ran away again, not even when Rebecca accidentally left the gate unlocked all night.

I learned something from Nick. Sometimes the most important thing a friend can do is simply be there. I may not be able to say comforting words when a friend loses her father, but my visit lets her know I care. Perhaps I can't help financially when a neighbor is unemployed, but I can share a cup of coffee and a silent prayer. And I can spend a few minutes each day sitting quietly in the presence of my best friend Jesus.

WAITING FOR FRIENDSHIP

Phyllis Hobe

Why won't he look at me?

For a month I had been working as a volunteer at a home for retarded children, and Jim—one of the children assigned to me—wasn't responding at all. Each time I visited, he simply stared at the television.

I tried everything. I showed him brightly colored balls, urged him to jump rope, offered him a bicycle to ride—but he only turned away. I worried incessantly about him . . . he was so alone, so friendless.

Then one day I brought my dog Trooper to work with me. Jim's eyes brightened the moment he saw the dog. Trooper sniffed all around Jim's room, the way dogs will, and once acquainted with his surroundings, he curled up at Jim's feet in front of the television set.

I left them together and went on to do other things.

When I returned an hour later, Trooper was peacefully curled up in Jim's lap, lying there quietly as Jim gently patted his head and whispered into his ear. They were friends!

Now why haven't I been able to draw some of that love from Jim? I asked myself. Because I had tried to force my friendship on him rather than simply let him be, as Trooper did, until he reached for me.

THE DUEL

Catherine Moore

atch out! You nearly broadsided that car!" my father yelled at me. "Can't you do anything right?!"

Those words hurt worse than blows. I turned my head toward the elderly man in the seat beside me, daring me to challenge him. A lump rose in my throat as I averted my eyes. I wasn't prepared for another battle.

"I saw the car, Dad. Please don't yell at me when I'm driving." My voice was measured and steady, sounding far calmer than I really felt. Dad glared at me, then turned away and settled back.

At home I left Dad in front of the television and went outside to collect my thoughts. Dark, heavy clouds hung in the air with a promise of rain. The rumble of distant thunder seemed to echo my inner turmoil. What could I do about him?

Dad had been a lumberjack in the great woods of Washington and Oregon. He'd enjoyed being outdoors and he'd reveled in pitting his strength against the forces of nature. He'd entered the grueling lumberjack competitions so popular in our area, and he had placed very often. The walls of his house were filled with trophies that attested to his prowess.

But the years marched on relentlessly. The first time he couldn't lift a heavy log he joked about it; but later that same day I saw him outside alone straining to lift it. He became irritable whenever anyone teased him about his advancing age or when he couldn't do something he had done as a younger man.

Four days after his sixty-seventh birthday he had had a heart attack. An ambulance sped him to the hospital while a paramedic administered CPR to keep blood and oxygen flowing to his brain. At the hospital Dad was rushed into an operating room. He was lucky; he survived.

But something inside Dad died. His zest for life was gone. He obstinately refused to follow doctor's orders. Suggestions and offers of help were turned aside with sarcasm and insults. The number of visitors thinned, then finally stopped altogether. Dad was left alone.

My husband, Dick, and I asked Dad to come live with us on our small farm. We hoped the fresh air and rustic atmosphere would help Dad adjust. Within a week after he moved in I regretted the invitation. It seemed nothing was satisfactory. He criticized everything I did. I became frustrated and moody. Soon I was taking my pent-up anger out on Dick. We began to bicker and argue. Alarmed, Dick sought out our pastor and explained the situation. The clergyman set up weekly counseling appointments for us. At the close of each session he prayed, asking God to soothe Dad's troubled mind. But the months wore on and God was silent.

A raindrop struck my cheek. I looked up into the dull, gray sky. Somewhere up there was "God." Although I believed a Supreme Being had created the universe, I had difficulty believing that "God" cared or even knew about the tiny human beings on this earth. And now I was tired of waiting for a God who didn't answer. Something had to be done and it was up to me to do it.

The next day I sat down with the phone book and methodically telephoned each of the mental-health clinics listed in the Yellow Pages. I explained my problem to each of the nameless, sympathetic voices that answered. In vain. Just when I was giving up hope, one of the voices suddenly exclaimed, "I just read something that might help you! Let me go get the article." Hardly daring to breathe, I listened as she read. The article described a remarkable study done at a nursing home. All of the patients were under treatment for chronic depression. Yet their attitudes, it seemed, had improved dramatically when they were given responsibility for a dog.

I hung up the telephone. A dog! Could anything as simple as a pet be the answer?

I drove to the animal shelter that very afternoon. After I filled out a questionnaire, the uniformed officer led me to the kennels. The odor of disinfectant stung my nostrils as I moved down the row of pens. Each contained some five to seven barking, leaping dogs of all descriptions. Longhaired dogs, curly-haired dogs, black dogs, spotted dogs—all jumped up, trying to reach me. I studied each one but mentally rejected one after the other for various reasons—too big; too small; too much hair, whatever. As I neared the last pen a dog in the shadows of the far corner struggled to his feet, walked to the front of the run and sat down. It was a pointer, one of the dog world's aristocrats. But this was a caricature of the breed. Years had etched his face and muzzle with shades of gray. His hipbones jutted out in lopsided triangles. But it was the eyes that caught and held my attention. Calm and clear, they beheld me unwaveringly.

I pointed to the dog. "Can you tell me about him?" The officer looked, then shook his head in puzzlement.

"He's a funny one. Appeared out of nowhere and sat in front of the gate. We brought him in figuring someone would be right down to claim him. That was two weeks ago and we've heard nothing. His time is up tomorrow." He gestured helplessly.

As the words sank in I turned to the man in horror. "You mean you're going to *kill* him?"

"Ma'am," he said gently, "that's our policy. We don't have room for every unclaimed dog."

I looked at the pointer again. The calm brown eyes awaited my decision. "I'll take him," I said impulsively.

I drove home with the dog on the front seat beside me. When I reached the house I honked twice. I was helping my prize out of the car when Dad shuffled onto the front porch.

"Ta-da! Look what I got for you, Dad!" I said excitedly.

Dad looked, then wrinkled his face in disgust, as though he had seen a particularly nasty species of insect. "If I had wanted a dog I would have gotten one. And I would have picked out a better specimen than that bag of bones. Keep it! I don't want it!" Dad waved his arm scornfully and turned back toward the house.

An anger rose inside me. It squeezed together my throat muscles, roared up to my head and pounded into my temples. I followed Dad, dragging the dog with me.

"You had better get used to him, Dad. He's staying!" Dad ignored me. "Did you hear me, Old Man?" I screamed. At those words Dad whirled angrily, his hands clenched tightly at his sides, his eyes narrowed and blazed with hate. We stood glaring at each other like duelists, tension creating an unbridgable chasm between us, when suddenly the pointer pulled free from my grasp. He wobbled toward my dad and sat down in front of him. Then slowly, carefully, he raised his right paw.

Dad's lower jaw trembled as he stared at the uplifted paw. Confusion replaced the anger in his eyes. The pointer waited patiently. Then Dad was on his knees hugging the animal.

It was the beginning of a warm and intimate friendship. Dad named the pointer Cheyenne. Together he and Cheyenne explored the community.

They spent long hours walking down dusty lanes. They spent reflective moments on the banks of streams, angling for tasty trout. They even started to attend Sunday services together, Dad sitting quietly in a pew and Cheyenne lying quietly at his feet.

Dad and Cheyenne were inseparable throughout the next three years. Dad's bitterness faded and he and Cheyenne made many friends. Then late one night I was startled to feel Cheyenne's cold nose burrowing through our bed covers. He had never before come into our bedroom at night! I woke Dick, put on my robe and ran into my father's room. Dad lay in his bed, his face serene. But his spirit had left quietly sometime during the night. As I stood staring at his peaceful expression, Dick came, checked my father's pulse, then gently guided me from the room.

Two days later my shock and grief deepened when I discovered Cheyenne lying dead beside Dad's bed. I wrapped his still form in the rag rug he had slept on beside Dad's bed. As Dick and I buried him near a favorite fishing hole, I silently thanked the dog for the help he had given me in restoring Dad's peace of mind.

The morning of Dad's funeral dawned overcast and dreary. *This day looks like the way I feel*, I thought as I walked down the aisle to the pews reserved for family. I was surprised to see the many friends Dad and Cheyenne had made filling the church. The pastor began his eulogy. It was a tribute to both Dad and the dog who had changed his life. And then the pastor turned to Hebrews 13:2. " 'Be not forgetful to entertain strangers, for thereby some have entertained angels unaware.' I've often thanked God for sending that angel," he said.

For me, the shadows of the past melded together and dropped into place, completing a puzzle that I had not seen before . . . the sympathetic voice that had just read the right article . . . Cheyenne's unexpected appearance at the animal shelter . . . his calm acceptance and complete devotion to my father . . . and the close proximity of their deaths. . . . And suddenly I understood, I *knew*, that God had answered my prayers after all.

REACHING OUT

Rick Hamlin

When my mother-in-law phoned us one evening to tell us about her new dog, I was surprised. "Another dog?" I said to my wife, Carol. "She already has three, McGhee, Siegfried and Butler . . . and now Missouri the Pug?"

But when we visited at my in-laws' home a week later and were greeted by this puppy wagging his tail so hard he almost fell over, licking our faces, his eyes shining with friendliness and trust, I soon relented.

Missouri *is* adorable. He stares at you through liquid eyes, furrowing his prematurely wrinkled brow, and when he jumps into your lap with his stumblebum paws . . . he's impossible to dismiss.

Since then, "Mo" and I have become great pals—going for walks, playing catch, shaking hands. But I'm especially grateful to Missouri for a very simple lesson he taught me. If ever I am uneasy about meeting strangers, I think of our first meeting. He didn't hesitate or hold back, waiting to see what I thought of him, if I wanted to be friends or not. No, he jumped right into my lap. He was instantly lovable because he instantly loved.

2

Acceptance

THE BIRD-FOOD THIEF

Deborah B. Schultz

My adventure began late in October when the air turned cold and crisp in western Connecticut. I am not particularly fond of winter, but one thing that brings me great pleasure and seems to lessen the chill is bird-watching. It was time to get the bird feeder out.

I hung the feeder—the type that dispenses sunflower seeds—on a hook in our backyard tree, where we would have a perfect view from all the back windows. It was also a convenient location for squirrels to help themselves to a feast, but I was not concerned because we hadn't been bothered by a single furry freeloader during the previous winter.

Birds have their own special radar and it takes only a day or two for them to home in on their favorite food. Sure enough, soon we were enjoying the usual visitors: chickadees, titmice and nuthatches. My daughters, Sarah, three, and Leah, one, were as delighted as I was to watch these lovely examples of God's creation. Bird-watching ended abruptly, however, the day I looked out to see a squirrel sitting in the feeder, gorging himself.

"Oh, no!" I yelled to my husband, David. "The squirrels have found the feeder."

"It's getting cold—they must be hungry too," my ever fair-minded husband replied.

"I wouldn't mind if he just took a seed or two, but he'll sit in there for hours," I wailed. "There won't be anything left for the birds."

"Squirrels are God's creatures, too," David persisted. "They need to eat."

Hmmmph, I thought to myself. *Squirrels have nuts and acorns to eat. I don't want them eating my sunflower seeds.* Meanwhile, Sarah and Leah were enjoying the sight of this little furry animal with the long bushy tail and the bright eyes. Sarah, with her child's innocence, forced me to look at him through different eyes. "He's so cute," she said with open admiration.

"Oh, all right," I said, feeling guilty about my dislike for the hungry creatures. "We'll feed the squirrels. But not sunflower seeds. We'll buy peanuts."

The next day I threw a handful of peanuts out in the yard, confident that the squirrels would be pleased and the birds would be able to return. I was even more satisfied to look out awhile later and see that the peanuts were gone. But my satisfaction quickly turned to dismay when I saw the squirrel sitting in the bird feeder quietly gorging himself once more.

Who had eaten the peanuts? I threw another handful out. *Swoop! Swoop! Swoop!* Down flew three huge black menacing-looking crows to snatch the peanuts up.

"I give up," I muttered to David when he came home. "Where did those crows come from? I've never seen crows around here before. And what are they doing eating peanuts? I thought they only ate . . . only ate . . . Well, you know, they're always in the streets scavenging."

"Crows are God's creatures, too," David calmly reminded me. He was beginning to sound like a stuck phonograph record.

"Forget it," I countered. "I'm not going to feed pesty squirrels and ugly crows." I marched outside, took the bird feeder down and put it in the garage.

A few days went by, days that seemed somehow colder, longer and emptier. I looked out the window a hundred times a day, but there were no birds to enjoy and no squirrels to yell at.

"I really miss the birds," I said to David. "I can't go all winter without them. Maybe I'll try a suet cage. The squirrels won't want that, I'm sure."

The hook in the tree was a perfect location for a suet cage, and within days we had two pairs of handsome redheaded woodpeckers feeding there. Then David surprised me by rigging a wire between two trees and hanging the sunflower seed feeder on it. The chickadees, titmice and nuthatches returned en masse.

I threw extra sunflower seeds on the ground, and these attracted cardinals, blue jays, mourning doves and even a tiny lone red squirrel, an uncommon species in our area. All this wonderful wildlife had me feeling quite magnanimous, and on the suggestion of a newspaper article, I put out piles of cracked corn for the squirrels.

I quickly discovered that the crows also enjoyed the corn but were fearful of coming close to the house. I placed some corn farther out in the yard and became thoroughly intrigued by watching them. My stereotype of crows is that they are big, ugly and mean. I was sure they would be aggressive, especially around food, and that they would attack anything that threatened their food supply. How wrong I was! To my surprise, I discovered that three large crows would sit *patiently* and wait—sometimes a half hour or more—until one relatively small squirrel was finished eating from "their" pile of corn. They wouldn't peck, they wouldn't caw. They waited, patiently and quietly.

It made me begin to think about my stereotypes of people. Like that mean-looking man who works at my local hardware store. I always rush in and out as fast as I can because I *assume* he'll snap at me if the children dare touch anything. Is it possible that he too is a quiet and patient man?

And the squirrels—yes, when they sit in the bird feeder, they're pesty in my eyes, but they play and share with each other; they rarely deny any of their kind a place at the feeding area; they really seem to *like* each other. I wish I could accept my fellow human beings as readily.

On the other hand, the blue jay, who is stunningly attractive with his bright blue plumage, is really quite selfish. Blue jays won't even share with each other and they always seem to be screeching. How often I've been taken in by someone's outer attractiveness, only to be disillusioned by his inner shallowness.

Late one afternoon Sarah was looking out the window when she asked, "What's that, Mommy?"

Thinking it was a new bird we hadn't seen before, I went to see what she had discovered.

"Oh, no," I exclaimed. An opossum was clinging to the suet cage, munching away to his heart's content. So much for my meditations during the past few weeks on hasty assumptions and stereotyping. I rushed headlong into judging and labeling. Based on looks alone—certainly not on facts—I told myself that the opossum on my suet cage, like all opossums, was greedy, ugly and sinister. I further assumed that the fuzzy creatures must have fuzzy brains because the only time I had ever seen one was after it had been hit by a car. With these thoughts uppermost in my mind, I ran out on the deck to scare the new visitor away. Yelling didn't work, and slamming a yardstick against the deck railing only broke the stick. Fortunately my mad impulse to throw stones went awry when my aim didn't even come close.

In a state of panic, I called my dad. (I knew David would only remind me about the opossum's being one of God's creatures.)

"What should you do?" Dad asked excitedly. "Get your camera, take some pictures, and you and the children watch him. You may never get such a wonderful opportunity again."

This was not the advice I was looking for. "What about the woodpeckers? They won't have any suet left. What if he attacks the cat?"

"He won't eat all the suet, and he certainly won't go near Schatzie. You're very lucky to have such a visit. Calm down and go enjoy it."

"Okay," I said in a sheepish voice.

Sarah and I watched the opossum for another hour, and when Leah woke from her nap she joined us. They oohed and aahed. When "Opie" departed—by now we had given him a nickname—he left more than enough suet for the woodpeckers, and I was struck by the effort and determination it took for him to get on and off the suet cage. He was slow-moving but certainly not lacking in intelligence or persistence. In the next few days I learned just how lucky we were to have seen such a creature up close and in the daylight. Opossums are nocturnal by nature and usually come out only at night.

Opie did return once more, again in daylight, and this second visit helped me feel forgiven for my initial reaction. I am ashamed when I think back on it, ashamed that I responded with instant dislike to something I knew nothing about. I wonder how often I have responded in a similar manner to people. How many times have I judged someone without first having gotten to know him or her? Can I change this aspect of myself?

I pray that I can and I thank God for the teachers He sent me that winter. His humble and wondrous creatures.

OUTSIZE PIGEON

The pigeon, huge atop the feeder meant
For cardinals and wrens and chickadees,
Maintains his roost precariously, intent
On small birds scattering sulkily through the trees,
Looking from them, with anxious puzzled longing,
To the little space below him where they fed;
Then, flapping toward the perch where they were thronging,
He lands indignantly on earth instead.
It takes a pigeon quite a while to learn
That one's endeavors and desires should be
Proportioned to the facts one can discern
(As it has, on occasion, taken me).
My sympathy goes with him as he flies
To find a place where he's the proper size.

—*Jane Merchant*

DILEMMA

Among the pink and blue of squills
And varied gold of daffodils
And gentle Eden-green of April grasses,
Outraging pastel innocence
With blackness startlingly intense,
A sinister, satanic starling passes.

He has no shadow of a right
To be there, evil to the sight.
I ought to chase him off, irate and snarling;
And yet, with all I've never done
To merit flowers, and grass, and sun,
Can I deny them even to a starling?

—*Jane Merchant*

Finding His Own Way

Phyllis Hobe

I couldn't wait. As soon as I arrived at the mountain cabin, I dashed down to the lake for a swim. My dog Trooper followed, his tail waving in exuberant circles as he eagerly sniffed the fresh country air.

Plunging into the water, I swam out to an old wooden raft to sun myself. But Trooper stood uncertainly at the water's edge.

"Trooper—come!" I called. It wasn't like him to hesitate. "Good boy, come on!"

He cocked his head questioningly and then ran in the opposite direction, disappearing into the thick bushes along the shore. I didn't like that and was about to tell him so when suddenly he leaped out of the bushes and plunged into the water, swimming straight for the raft. He climbed aboard and stood wagging his whole body as though he expected me to praise him. *For what?* I wondered.

Then I studied the shore again and saw that the bushy area was much closer to the raft than the sandy beach from where I had entered the water. Trooper hadn't been disobedient after all—he was simply looking for a shorter route.

"Good boy!" I said, patting his head. "Good, *good* boy!"

Make Up Your Mind, Oreo!

Arthur Gordon

T his morning our big cat, Oreo (so named because he is a handsome black-and-white), and I go through a familiar ritual at the back door.

Oreo has been outside for a while and he really wants to come in. So I open the door and wait. But will he come in? No, he won't. He stops and lowers his head suspiciously, as if I were some deadly enemy. "Come on, Oreo," I say impatiently.

He sits down thoughtfully and begins to wash his face with one paw. Maddening.

"Oreo," I say, "I give you food. I supply all your needs. If you do anything in return, I don't know what it is. Now I'm personally inviting you into my house. So come on in!"

Oreo puts one foot across the threshold, then draws it back. He looks out across the yard with some remote, unfathomable expression. He still doesn't come in.

"Oreo," I say, "I'm not going to stand here forever. If you don't come in, I'm going to close this door. This is your last chance!"

I start to close the door slowly. Does he come in? No, he sits there, exercising his free will or something. He'll come when it suits him, not before. He figures I'll be patient. So far, he's right.

God made cats. He also made people. I wonder how He feels, sometimes, when He stands at the door and waits . . . and waits . . .

I think I know.

ON HIS OWN TERMS

Marjorie Holmes

*W*here Tiger came from we'll never know, nor where he goes when we're away. He simply sprang from the hedges one night when we drove in from our weekend at the lake, a striped gray tom, howling as if to demand, "Where have you *been?*" and entwining our legs like long-lost kin.

Because of our two dogs, we fed and bedded Tiger on the porch, thinking he'd surely be gone in a few days. But he promptly took up residence. And our instant, abiding love for him has never waned.

So it was with some regret that we left for a month's vacation that first year. Margaret, our next-door neighbor, agreed to feed him, but we doubted Tiger would be there when we returned. And sure enough it was true.

"Sorry about your cat," Margaret told us. "He hung around for a couple of days, then disappeared."

But as we stood mourning the inevitable, who should come scurrying up to purr his forgiveness and welcome but Tiger?

And thus it has been for almost four years. Mysteriously, he senses our homecoming. And no matter how long we may have stayed away, he comes rushing upon us, showing in every way he can how much he loves us, and how glad he is to have us home.

Lord, no matter how far from You we stray, or how long we may be gone, You always faithfully await our return.

"You Can Stay"

Sue Monk Kidd

*L*ast week a friend called saying he had a "precious" beagle puppy looking for a home. Say puppy to me and I lose all reason. I saw a small, droopy-eared creature with big brown eyes that said, "Love me." I didn't consider the headaches that come with new puppies. "We'll take him," I heard myself say.

Within forty-eight hours he had deprived me of sleep with all-night whimpering, shredded the cover on a coffee table book, gnawed a hole in my draperies and made a disaster of the carpet. Suddenly he didn't seem so "precious." He fell more into the category of an Egyptian plague.

"What am I going to do with you?" I said, staring into his brown-and-white face. He cocked his head at me. And once again those eyes seemed to say, "Love me."

As I picked him up, I couldn't help but think how my experience with this pup was not so different from my interaction with people. Sometimes I reached out to them with a surge of emotion. But when I came in contact with their imperfections and discovered the nuisance side of their nature, I wanted to back away. Yet love, I reminded myself, meant taking the bad along with the good.

The puppy licked my nose. "All right," I told him. "You can stay."

Forgiving the Runaway

Marjorie Holmes

*L*et him go," my husband, George, declared as Ben streaked away through the drizzling darkness the minute the car had stopped. "Let's unpack and go to bed. Never again will we go looking for him the way we did when he disappeared last summer." And carrying luggage into the cottage, putting things away, we went through our usual dialogues of despair about that dog, treated so handsomely, yet escaping whenever our backs are turned.

George fell asleep at once. I lay awake, pondering the strange ways of some creatures: dogs who seem to love you, yet have no loyalty and can't be trusted; while others can't be lured from your side. *There are people like that too*, I thought. And whether it's dogs or human beings, we feel hurt by such behavior. Yet dogs don't do these things consciously; they are blindly unaware of betrayal. This dog was driven by his instincts, perhaps the scent of a female in the distance, perhaps simply his need for freedom after hours in the car.

Around midnight I heard his bark at the door. By then it was raining, the wind blowing, thunder booming, lightning stabbing the swaying trees. Ben stood there boldly demanding shelter, exhibiting no shame. "He came back only because of the storm," we agreed, as I let him in. "How would *he* feel if we said, 'No, stay out there, we don't want you any more'?"

But we also agreed: "How would we feel if we turned him away?"

Yet Ben must have felt guilty, for he slunk into the kitchen the next morning and lay eyeing me as if doubtful about his breakfast. I had only to say, "You don't deserve anything, you were a bad dog last night!" for him to scurry off as if struck, and to lie mournful, head on his paws.

We fed him, of course. We petted and forgave him, the way we always do . . .

The way God forgives us when we forget how good He is to us, how much He loves us, and run away.

3
Trust

"God Will See to It"

Don Bell

I watched my little mare day and night. She was due to foal at any time, and I wanted this foal more than any horse I'd ever dreamed of. A cowboy loves a good horse, and the only way to get one is to breed your best mare to a stallion who can provide you with the horse of your dreams.

It was early spring in high-altitude country, so I kept my mare in a box stall bedded with good bright straw. On cool nights I put a horse blanket over her, and several times a night I would take a flashlight and go down to check on her. I really did worry about this mare and the foal she was carrying.

One afternoon when the weather seemed nice I turned the mare loose in a small horse pasture so that she could get some exercise. Then a neighbor dropped by to ask me to go with him to his ranch to help him mend some fences, so I did. While I was there an angry-looking storm came up. I got more and more nervous about my mare, and told my friend I had to get back to her. He was a rugged old rancher who just smiled. He said, "God will see to it that she has her foal when the right time comes. Your being there won't help her a bit!"

Sure enough, when I got back home after dark and ran with my flashlight to check on the mare, there she stood at the corral gate with a fine sorrel colt at her side.

I learned something from that: to trust God more and "lean unto my own understanding" less.

LEO THE LIONHEARTED

Susan DeVore Williams

First, you should know that this isn't just another cat story. The main character is, I admit, my Siamese cat, Leo. I can't tell you that Leo ever dragged me from a burning building or croaked his deafening Siamese meow to warn me of an impending earthquake. But God has used him to teach me a lesson it's taken me twenty years to learn, and not many cats can be *that* kind of hero.

From the moment our eyes met through the pet shop window in Minneapolis on a cold spring day in 1964, I knew this sealpoint kitten was something special. He struggled and protested loudly as the shopkeeper pulled him from his cage.

"He may be small," I laughed, "but he seems to have the heart of a lion."

"He has the voice of a lion, too," the shopkeeper said. And so I named him Leo the Lionhearted. Even his birthday seemed symbolic. Valentine's Day.

My husband and I were childless and, as often happens, we became more than casually attached to Leo. He managed to fit himself into every area of our lives effortlessly and completely. I grew to expect his noisy greeting at the door each evening, and enjoyed his flattering, rapt attention when I wandered around our apartment doing housework. He even developed an awareness of my moods, pawing at my leg to be picked up when he sensed I needed comforting, then patting my cheek with his paw.

Sometimes I'd catch myself carrying on an animated conversation with Leo as he'd perch on a chair and gaze at me. "If I could be that kind of listener," I told him, "I'd be the most popular woman in town." And Leo never disagreed with me.

In his third year, Leo stayed with my parents while we were away on an extended business trip. When we picked him up he was listless and very thin. My father had tried everything to coax him to eat, to no avail. His belly seemed bloated, and within a few hours it had grown so large he had trouble sitting down. I called his veterinarian. "Bring him to my office now," he said.

At the clinic, the vet made a quick diagnosis: a kidney stone. "Another hour and he'll be dead unless I take some emergency measures. I don't guarantee anything. He's in a lot of pain. Do you want me to go ahead and catheterize him, or should I put him to sleep?"

I stood in numbed silence. Words wouldn't come. Finally, I shook my head. "Do what you can to save him. Please."

I sat in the waiting room until, at long last, the vet returned. "I don't know what to tell you. I've catheterized him, but he's passed another stone, and I'm afraid this is going to be a chronic problem. He needs surgery, and I doubt he'll survive it. He's very underweight and weak. If it were my cat, I'd put him to sleep."

"Does he have any chance at all for recovery?" I asked.

"I'd say no," the vet said. "I'm sorry, but I know you want the truth. He may have a five or ten percent chance of surviving surgery, but he will always have this problem."

"I need some time alone with him, please," I managed to say.

When the vet left me in the examining room, I stroked Leo's fragile body and watched him breathe. Until that moment I hadn't realized how much I'd come to love my lionhearted cat.

"Lord, I can't kill him unless You tell me to," I said aloud. "You're going to have to give me some sort of confirmation, or else You're going to have to do it Yourself. Show me, Lord." I waited.

Perhaps five minutes passed, and I stood stroking Leo's head. He was very still. Suddenly, a thought entered my head: *Pray for him. Pray for his healing.* I laughed bitterly. "Pray for an animal? I'm really cracking up!"

After a few moments, my heart racing, I put both hands on Leo's body. "In the name of Jesus, you are whole. In life or in death, you belong to God. I commit your spirit to God, who created you." I paused. "Father, I ask You for Leo's life. Please restore him to health. Thank You, Lord. I trust You with his life."

The vet walked into the room as if on cue, looking expectantly at me.

"I want you to operate," I told him. "Do whatever you can to get him through the night. I'll talk with you in the morning."

"Okay," he said reluctantly. "But I don't think he'll survive the surgery."

By morning, as I prayed, my faith was about half the size of a mustard seed. I dreaded calling the vet.

"Well, sometimes animals will surprise you," he said. "He made it through the night. But he's a very, very sick cat. I can't give you any real hope. Do you want to see him?"

Leo was an even more pitiful sight than he'd been the night before. I should have let him be put to sleep. But deep within, I could feel God's gentle reproof: *Where is your faith? You asked Me for restoration. Trust Me!*

I stroked Leo's head and he slowly raised his eyes to my face.

Oh, Lord, I thought, *he trusts me so completely. Even in this pain, he trusts me. I want to be like that with You. Help me trust You in my pain. Make me like that, Lord!*

I moved my hand under Leo's throat and ever so faintly I felt a vibration. He was purring.

The following morning, the vet called to warn me that Leo was now only four pounds, would not eat at all, and would have to be force-fed if he was to survive even another day. "It might give him an extra will to live if you took him home," he said. "Being in familiar surroundings might help."

Hastily, I prepared for Leo's return: padded box with a heating pad, bottles of baby food, eye droppers for liquids.

"Okay, Lord," I said on the drive to pick him up. "It's up to You."

Through the next twenty-four hours I attempted to feed Leo every fifteen minutes. Because he was unable even to lick water, I squirted it into the side of his mouth. Most of it dribbled out onto the towel I'd wrapped around him. He gazed at me with unblinking eyes. I scraped baby food onto his lower teeth, but it simply lay on his gums. Finally I sat beside Leo unmoving, weariness sapping my strength, and I said, "Lord, should I stop? Show me. I need to know Your desire, Your intentions."

I put one more fingerful of food to Leo's mouth, and started to open his lips. Then I watched his tongue slowly reach out and lick the food from his teeth, and then from my finger. I let out a whoop and jumped to my feet.

I had an impulse to read a Psalm of thanksgiving and I reached for my Amplified Bible. Leafing randomly through Psalms, I began to read aloud, not really thinking deeply about the words, until they began to sink in as I reached verse 10. "For every beast of the forest is mine and the cattle upon a thousand hills or upon the mountains where thousands are. I know and am acquainted with all the birds of the mountains, and the wild animals of the field are mine, and are with me, in my mind" (50:10–12).

Stunned, I read the words again and again, feeling the heaviness lift from my heart. "Lord, how wonderful You are," I prayed. "Leo's Yours, and he's always in Your mind. Thank You for lending him to me, for making him my trusting friend. Thank You for showing me that I need to be that kind of trusting friend to You."

Within forty-eight hours, Leo was walking shakily and eating normally. In a week, he was recovering. In three months, his weight was up to nine pounds.

"Just don't expect this to be permanent," the vet told me when I took Leo for a checkup. "At any moment, he could get another kidney stone, and that'll be it."

Over the next two years I rejoiced in Leo's good health. But I also developed a kind of chronic fear as a result of the vet's dismal prognosis. I watched Leo daily for signs of recurrence. If he sneezed, I called the vet. Finally, toward the middle of his fifth year, it happened: the same symptoms, but I caught them before the bloating got out of hand. In a state of panic, I raced to the vet.

By this time, fear had a good grip on me. "Lord," I said, "is this it? Two short years? I thought You'd healed him completely." I felt a pang of guilt. I wasn't doing a very good job of trusting God, I thought. *No*, I could feel the Lord saying deep inside, *you aren't.*

It turned out that Leo had a serious infection, and he nearly died again.

Leo recovered, of course. And in his seventh and ninth and twelfth years, he had similar brushes with death. Each time, my confidence in God's intentions grew. But the fear didn't leave entirely. I prayed over and over that God would remove it.

In Leo's sixteenth year, we moved to California. There, my life entered a phase that hardly seemed real. My husband of eighteen years left me. But I got "custody" of Leo. Once again, he spent long hours at my side, comforting me with his presence.

Then, just a few weeks after my husband's departure, Leo developed symptoms of infection. "No, Lord!" I cried. "I can't go through this now! Don't take him away from me! Don't do this!" Fear seemed more powerful than ever. I was so distraught that without pausing to think, I found myself speaking in a loud, angry voice: "Stop it! Just stop."

Who—or what—was I speaking to?

Fear, I thought. That's what.

"Stop," I said again, angrier than ever. "Fear, I am sick of you. This cat doesn't belong to me. He belongs to God. The Lord has healed and restored him over and over again, when everyone said it was hopeless. So it's time you just got *lost.*"

Amazed at my own words, I smiled. And then I felt it. The fear *had* departed. I was calm. I gathered up my lionhearted cat and told him, "Don't worry. You're going to be fine. As usual."

But that night, as I lay in bed, the emotional pain of my broken marriage began to overwhelm me. Leo would be all right, I knew, but what about me? I was nearly forty, without any kind of support system in this strange city. I had no future, no career, no money, no home, and my friends and family were more than two thousand miles away. "Lord," I whispered into the night, "what will become of me? I'm so *afraid*."

Leo padded from the foot of the bed toward my face. His cold nose touched my chin. In the darkness, he settled down to comfort me again.

"Leo, I'm so scared," I told him. "I'm so *scared*." He purred and licked my cheek. Slowly, the truth began to dawn on me.

God had taught me to trust Him for my cat's life. It had taken most of Leo's proverbial nine lives to do it. Each time he'd approached the brink of death and all had seemed hopeless, God had done the impossible. I could almost hear Him say, "How many times are you going to have to go through this before you finally learn to trust Me?"

Yet God had done the same things in my life that He'd done in Leo's! Events crowded through my mind as incident after incident played out like a movie. Time and again the Lord had met my need—and in ways I'd never expected. Had He ever abandoned me? Had He ever failed to provide food, clothing, shelter, work, friends and everything else I needed? Had He ever broken His promises?

I hugged Leo close. "We're going to be okay," I whispered.

And we were.

Valentine's Day 1984 was Leo's twentieth birthday. He's had skirmishes with death in the last four years, but the fear has not returned. His new vet pronounces him one of the Seven Wonders of the World.

"He's probably your oldest friend," the vet said on her last visit to check Leo. "It's going to be terribly difficult for you when he finally goes."

I thought about that. Yes, it will be hard. It can't be anything else. But the fear—well, we've gotten through that together, Leo and I. And we've learned about trusting God, together. The Bible told me that Leo is always in God's mind and, in a loving and miraculous way, God has revealed His mind to me through this lionhearted cat.

I scratched Leo's ears and smiled. The vet stroked him admiringly.

"I'll say this for him," she said. "He's sure lived up to his name."

Editor's note: Leo lived another year, to the ripe cat age of twenty-one. He died of old age just three days after his birthday.

FOLLOWING THE VOICE

Marion Bond West

My husband, Gene, and I walked through our two pastures. We wanted the exercise, so we moved at a rapid pace. Our golden retriever, Elmo, ran ahead, excited. The grass was tall and the walking a bit rough. Several times I thought I heard a faint meow and we stopped, thinking there might be a stray kitten around. As we neared the end of our walk, something over a mile, I distinctly heard a loud meow. Gene, Elmo and I stopped and listened. In the distance we saw a familiar figure jump up out of the tall grass, almost like a rabbit. It was our tiny bobtail kitten! She'd followed us all this distance, running to keep up. She must have frequently popped up out of the grass, which was well over a foot high, to determine our location.

"Oh, Bobbie," I cried, running back to her and lifting her to my shoulder. Usually a finicky kitten, she now nuzzled her head against me like a relieved child. I could feel her heart pounding. She licked my hands as I carried her back to the house, and she purred all the way.

Walking home, I thought, *I ought to be more like Bobbie.* Whatever my fear or need, from now on I will run straight toward the sound of God's voice, knowing that I am wanted and will be shown safely home.

"I WANT TO BE NEAR YOU"

Cora Peters

Our cat Lu-Lu recently had surgery. She is recuperating nicely but is still unable to jump around with her usual ease. This morning as I was having a cup of coffee and reading my devotional, she put her paws on my chair and attempted to leap onto my lap. She jumped part way and fell backward. To me, she seemed to be saying, "I want to be near you. Please help me up."

I tried to hoist her up, but she stiffened in pain. For some reason, I thought of how God works in my life. Sometimes I'm in pain, not so much physically but mentally as I agonize over some decision I have to make. I want God to be near, but my troubles make Him seem far away.

Thinking of Lu-Lu again, I moved from my chair down onto the floor next to her. She moved easily into my lap. Lu-Lu curled up happily, contentedly, and went to sleep. Her reaction made me realize that I need not struggle to be near God; I can merely reach out to Him, and He lovingly comes to embrace me with His presence.

USING OUR WINGS

Carolyn F. Young

When I first saw the pelican, he was fishing for his dinner in the boiling waters that rush down from Montana's Fort Peckham Dam. He must have known the danger that surrounded him, for at any moment he could be dashed against one of the high walls toward which a relentless current kept pushing him.

It became a habit with me to stop and watch my friend, the pelican. His superb indifference to the turmoil about him intrigued me—perhaps because I was, myself, struggling in a rather rough sea of personal difficulty. I watched him ride serenely on top of the seething, troubled water and I longed to imitate his poise.

"O God," I prayed, "if only I could do that . . ." I watched closer. When the walls loomed too near, the pelican lifted his strong wings, flew briefly out of the cauldron, and a moment later returned again. As long as his wings were strong enough to fly him from the rock wall, he could live in that beating water and go about his business.

The moment this thought formed itself in my mind, a tingle moved down my spine for I realized the pelican, himself, had provided the answer to my half-formed prayer: yes, I too had *wings*—only I had forgotten how to use them.

Ever since then, whenever life's tensions become too threatening, I simply fly away—for a moment—like the pelican, on my own strong wings of prayer. Then I come back to the storm-tossed sea again, renewed and refreshed.

DETERMINED SCRATCHING

Marion Bond West

As I stood at my kitchen sink one day, my thoughts were nearly paralyzed by a problem that I couldn't seem to solve. The problem was too big . . . I was too small. Surely God wouldn't have any interest in it. Engulfed in self-pity and doubt, I decided not to even approach my Father.

I leaned forward and stared out the window, tense and miserable. Then a slight movement caught my eye. Scratching around there in the dry leaves on the ground was a young brown wood thrush, determined to unearth a tasty morsel. He refused to abandon his busy efforts even though he obviously wasn't finding any food. Not even one tiny bug. *Scratch, scratch, scratch,* the tiny sounds continued.

"Oh!" I cried softly. Just as I had heard the little thrush's attempts to fulfill his needs, why wouldn't my Father hear my pleas too? I ran outside with a bag of birdseed and filled the empty feeder. Back in the house and once more at the window, I watched the tiny bird light on the feeder and begin to feast hungrily. Still watching him, my small, scratchy prayer began—

Father, O Father . . .

JOY
(IN THE MIDDLE OF GRIEF)

Like sparrows in the winter
We dream of spring;
Meanwhile,
Incredibly sustained
By drapeless sky,
By balded bough,
And crumbs,

WE SING!

And strangely exultant,
Wing the unpaved way
Men call today.

— *Sallie Chesham*

SUNSET THRUSH

Perhaps he was not praying,
The sunset thrush I heard.
Perhaps he was not saying
His thanks; perhaps a bird
In leafy dimness swaying
Can have no thought of prayer;
But my own heart is praying
Because I heard him there.

—*Jane Merchant*

4

Helping

DROP SEED

Sue Monk Kidd

*M*onday. From the window I notice a small brown wren huddled on the grass beneath the bird-feeder, struggling to fly. The frigid wind bends the branches of the crabapple tree. Fifteen minutes pass. He cannot seem to find the strength. Is he sick? Too young? Too weak? It seems sad. But I suppose there is little I can do for him.

Suddenly my attention is drawn to another wren that flies to the feeder. I am astonished as she begins to toss seed with her beak from the ledge of the feeder down to the grass below. It falls like kernels of grace upon the little bird, satisfying his hunger. The next time I pass the window he's gone.

Tuesday. I watch the wrens pecking at the feeder, thinking of the lesson they have taught me. We are put here not only to partake, but to feed the hungers of those around us. I look at the feeder. *Drop seed*, God whispers. *Drop seed.*

The Loving Neighbors
Aletha Jane Lindstrom

In an attempt to "bring back the bluebird," my husband and I maintain fifty nesting boxes near our Lake Michigan cottage. This past summer we were delighted when a pair of these lovely, endearing birds settled into a box in our backyard.

Then one morning, shortly after five babies hatched, I found the male dead by the roadside, apparently struck while fluttering down for insects to feed his young. Heartsick, I picked up the small, limp, still-warm body. The loss of even one of these endangered birds is a tragedy. Surely this was a double tragedy, for the mother alone could never feed her hungry brood.

That evening the unbelievable happened. A pair of bluebirds from a nearby field and their five nearly grown fledglings appeared on the back fence. Daily from dawn till dusk they helped the widowed mother feed her nestlings. They stayed even after the babies were out of the box to assist in training them to become self-sufficient. At summer's end they migrated together.

Love thy neighbor? These gentle, unassuming birds *lived* their love.

Lost and Found
Phyllis Hobe

I enjoy watching the wild geese fly over my house. Some of the largest flocks in the country come every winter to feed in the cornfields near my home, and I see them several times a day. Recently I learned that these migrant birds actually travel by night and during the day they are busy foraging for food—all of which explains something that happened recently one dark night.

My dog Kate and I were walking across a field when I heard a goose's forlorn honking overhead. I squinted into the night sky but couldn't see anything. There was only the sound of a pair of large wings circling above—and those sad cries.

Then I heard the call of other geese far in the distance—not from the sky but from somewhere on the ground. With that, the wings circling over my head began to beat faster and the anxious crying became louder. Then the bird flew off toward the call of the distant geese and I heard a joyful mingling of honks rise from the darkness of the farther field. The lost goose was found! Somehow he must have become separated from his flock during their night journey and, his cries heard, his family had come to guide him back to their midst.

I walked home with a happy heart because I too know what it is to lose my way. And I too know the joy of hearing God's voice guiding me to the safety of His loving care. He never asks why or how I lost my way. He is just happy to have me back.

THE DOG WHO WAS THERE

Hazel Houston

One day a dog appeared at our Iowa farm. Somehow we understood that he had come to stay. We fed him table scraps, but he did not beg for food as some dogs do, nor did he wag his tail with happiness when fed.

He did not have a distinctive coloring. His hair was brown mixed with black, his tail stubby. We did not even give him a name, perhaps because he never had to be called. He was always there. This dog seemed to think his mission in life was to accompany me as I went about the outdoor duties of a farmwife. When I fed the chickens or gathered vegetables, he was by my side. Sometimes, not only did he escort me, but he also carried one of my hands gently in his mouth.

One day a stranger came. Oddly, he parked his car midway between the house and the barn. When I stepped out on the porch, he asked a question about the previous owner of our farm. Then he appeared not to hear my answer. He walked toward me and asked the question again. This time I walked out in the yard a short way before I answered him. Again he seemed not to understand and continued to walk toward me. Now I sensed that he could hear me perfectly well.

Suddenly the man came to an abrupt stop. "Will that dog bite?" he asked.

I had not realized the dog was beside me, so quietly had he come. This time he did not take my hand in his mouth. His upper lip was pulled back revealing sharp teeth.

"He certainly will," I answered firmly.

The man understood my words perfectly. He hurried to his car and drove away.

Soon after, the dog left. He may have gone to hunt rabbits and just never came back.

Somehow I do not think so.

My Good
and Faithful Friends

Mary Gladys Baker

"Hi, Mom!" My daughter, Dale, greeted me when I finally limped my way to the ringing telephone. "I just wanted to remind you that the basketball game starts at six-thirty."

I might be old and forgetful, but there wasn't much chance I'd forget that the University of Oklahoma was playing Louisiana State on television that night last January. Lord knows, when you're eighty-four years old and have outlived your husband and half your friends, you find your pleasure where you can. And I found basketball, particularly Oklahoma basketball, a real source of pleasure.

"Thanks for calling," I said to Dale as I glanced at the ice on the kitchen window and at the snow-shrouded dusk beyond. "I'm warm as July and ready for the tip-off."

Now, I knew that Dale hadn't really called to remind me about the game. She'd called to check on me. Not that I minded. I'd had eleven surgeries and enough strokes to leave my left leg dragging. Sometimes I felt the same as that left leg, dragging and worthless.

I went to the back door. Little Bit, my ten-month-old Labrador retriever, followed me as I looked for a glimpse of Scout, her seven-year-old counterpart who ruled the backyard and hated to be inside. Scout's bed was protected from the snow on a covered patio, but with the setting of the sun the temperature dropped fast. I figured now was as good a time as any to replace Scout's damp quilt with the dry one I had stored above his bed. I'd give him his bedtime cookie, too. Both my dogs loved cookies, particularly vanilla creams.

I put on a pair of old tennis shoes without laces. "Stay inside!" I ordered Little Bit as I stepped out the door. The bitter wind whipped through my nightgown as I hurried across the patio toward Scout's wagging tail. And there, suddenly, I slipped.

The hard concrete of the patio jarred the breath out of me. I opened my eyes with a moan and tried to sit up, but I couldn't move my legs. I ran a shaking hand across my left hip, where a hard knot jutted out at an awkward angle. I'd broken my hip! *Stay calm. Think.*

Scout wandered over and sniffed me. His cold nose assured me that this wasn't a nightmare. Shivering, I looked around for help, but my eyes weren't focusing right. I reached up and touched my face and realized my glasses were gone. Squinting, I saw them across the patio, where the force of my fall had thrown them.

The only sound I heard was the wind crackling in the frozen trees. Eerie light from the television flickered through the window, casting marauding images on the snow. I shivered as much from fear as from the cold. How long before someone would find me? Dale had already called this evening. Everyone was buttoned up at home thinking I was watching the game. No one would check on me until tomorrow. *God, help me! I can't survive out here all night.*

"Help! Help! Somebody help me!" I screamed, even though nobody could hear. Scout raised his ears with curiosity, then huddled back and curled into a ball on his bed. I looked at the back door— fifteen feet and one glass storm door was all that separated me from warmth. With a determined effort I struggled again to sit up. No use. I raised up on my elbow and looked around. Scout's chain! It was thirty feet long and connected to a patio post. I pushed myself onto my side and reached for the chain. I had it!

Holding the chain with both hands, I closed my eyes and pulled, dragging myself along inch by inch. Pausing to catch my breath, I opened my eyes to check my progress only to find that the chain was pulling me *away* from the door! I choked back my frustration, propped myself on one elbow and began dragging myself in the right direction. There were three steps leading up to the door with a low railing beside them. If I could reach that railing, maybe I could pull myself up the steps.

I felt sand grinding into my elbow as I moved. My tennis shoes fell off, causing my heels and ankles to scrape against the concrete. "Thank You, Lord, that there's no ice on the patio," I whispered.

The effort of pulling myself warmed me a bit as I inched toward the door. I almost shouted when I reached the railing beside the steps. I reached up and pulled, then pulled again, but pull as I might, I couldn't lift myself up the stairs. I'd gone as far as I could.

Loneliness covered me like a cloak. All those years of frantic bustling raising young'uns had faded into long hours of passing time. How much time did I have left? It was hard, sometimes, to be beholden to people, but I'd never experienced total helplessness before.

"God, I've done all I can do. Please don't let me freeze to death," I prayed through chattering teeth.

Little Bit, whimpering, watched me through the storm door. I was close enough to see her now, even without my glasses. Barking, she hurled herself against the door. Again and again she threw herself against the glass until, finally, the door flew open. She bounded down the steps and crouched beside me, laying her cheek against mine. Warm breath panted against my frozen face.

"Good girl, Little Bit," I crooned, trying hard to swallow the lump in my throat. Little Bit licked my cheek, then, as if assured that I was alive, ran off to play with my glasses. Scout wandered over and curled up behind my back. I could feel his heart thumping against my spine; the rhythm of his breathing was hypnotic. Soon the sighs of his sleep mixed with the sound of the wind.

Sleep. I'd always heard that freezing people should never go to sleep. They might not wake up. My face felt blistered by the cold, my elbows screamed with pain, but worse, I couldn't feel the cold on my feet.

I tried to imagine the hottest day I could remember. Those days before air conditioning, sweltering in the Oklahoma sun. Only I couldn't. I couldn't remember anything except the cold that chilled my very core. How long had I been there? I looked at the familiar sky and guessed it was after midnight.

The wind picked up, its gusts slapping me with icy fingers that lifted my gown, shooting pain down my leg. I gasped for breath as the wind whipped across the snow, stinging my face with ice crystals.

Jesus! The cry came from deep inside of me. "Jesus." Just whispering the name made me feel stronger. How long had I been trusting that name? Was it fifty years or sixty now? Years of reading the Bible and attending the Church of Christ . . .

So, was this what it had come down to? Me meeting my Maker by freezing to death? I thought of my oldest daughter fighting her deadly battle against cancer. None of it made any sense. Her having cancer while an old woman like me just kept hanging on. Yet something deep inside me clung to life.

Suddenly I remembered the Scripture Paul wrote while he was in prison waiting to die: "I also suffer these things: nevertheless I am not ashamed: for I know him whom I have believed" (2 Timothy 1:12). The words took on new meaning as I repeated them aloud.

"Father God," I prayed, "I'm suffering out here in this cold, and I don't believe You'll let me freeze to death. I'm trusting You to save me, but whether I live or die, I believe in Jesus."

A few minutes later Scout stirred, then stood and began walking away, removing my only shield from the north wind. The wind blasted my back, and my body began jerking so hard I could barely talk. "Scout, come back, boy. Come back and lie down." He paused and looked back at me, then trotted toward his bed.

I watched in amazed silence as Scout sank his teeth into the corner of the quilt on his bed, backed up and began pulling the blanket across the patio. Little Bit pranced around while Scout tugged the quilt over my body.

"Good boy, Scout!" I sobbed, pulling the damp quilt up around my shoulders and tucking it under my elbow. The quilt, tattered and potted with holes, blocked the buffeting wind. Scout lay down and stretched his long body beside my back, radiating warmth like warm coals.

I raised my head to check on Little Bit. If only I had my glasses. *Ask her.* The thought came unbidden.

"Little Bit, could you bring my glasses?" Little Bit trotted across the patio, picked up my glasses and brought them to me. *Thank You, Jesus.*

My broken hip was numb, but my leg felt like raw nerves exposed to the cold. What I wouldn't give for a hot water bottle or a heating pad. *Ask Little Bit.*

What a strange thought. Little Bit can't go inside and get my heating pad . . . Of course, she probably feels as warm as Scout . . . and she did get my glasses . . .

"Little Bit, come here, girl. Look at my legs. Could you lie down right here on my left leg?" Her liquid eyes met and held mine for a moment before she lay gently where I had asked her. Warmth from her body radiated through the damp blanket, creating moist heat that seeped into the bone, easing my pain. I felt cradled between the dogs, their satiny black coats a vivid contrast to the moonlit snow. Blood began pulsating through my frozen limbs as if answering the rhythm of their heartbeats.

"Little Bit, you and Scout are going to get as many cookies as you want when I get back on my feet."

I watched clouds drifting in the night sky while I talked to God, Scout and Little Bit. The first rays of sunrise cast a crimson flush over the snow, bringing several degrees of instant warmth. The sun was high in the morning sky when I heard a car stop by my mailbox.

"Help!" I croaked, my hoarse voice barely above a whisper. I heard the door open and knew Dale had gone into the house. "O Lord, You've brought me through the night. Please don't let Dale leave without finding me."

"Mother!" Dale screamed when she saw me. Soon I was loaded into an ambulance that headed to Wichita Falls, Texas, as if its tail were on fire. I had surgery to repair my broken hip but refused surgery to amputate my frostbitten heels. During the fifteen days in the hospital, as my damaged heel peeled off in layers and fresh new baby skin took its place, it seemed as if my whole life had been peeled away and made fresh.

When I came home again, I thought back to the story of Balaam in the Old Testament and how God used a donkey to save him from the angel of death. I smiled as I handed Scout and Little Bit yet another vanilla cream. If God could use dogs and donkeys, I guess He still has use for an old gal like me.

Jocko—At Your Service

Marilyn Mesi Pona

I'll never forget what it was like to be disabled. And to need a helpful companion at my side.

Some time back I suffered through six years of intense back pain. Scoliosis had deformed my right hip and put me first on crutches, then in a wheelchair. I'd always been an active person, and losing my mobility was frustrating. I was constantly dropping socks and pens and utensils that were impossible for me to pick up. My life was strewn with objects I couldn't reach, doors I couldn't maneuver through, tiny chores I couldn't manage. My husband and three children helped me as much as possible, but they couldn't be with me all the time.

At last, doctors operated and removed pieces of ruptured disks that had twisted a nerve in my spine. The excruciating pain was gone. I could walk again! I went home, thanking God for my recovery.

But the energy I had mustered to fight the pain swirled inside me with no place to go. My children were growing up and busy with activities of their own; my husband had his job. Now what would fill *my* time?

I tried gardening, joined clubs, volunteered at animal shelters, took walks with my Labrador retriever, Max. But nothing challenged me. I couldn't help feeling there was some project that I was meant to do. I'd prayed for help during my time of pain, and I prayed now for guidance.

And then a news item about Sandy Maze of Columbus, Ohio, appeared on television. Sandy, who had muscular dystrophy, had paid a trainer to teach her dog, Stormy, to help her with simple but important tasks, such as retrieving keys, pencils and other objects. With Stormy's help, Sandy had been able to get around on her own, to lead a fuller, richer life, and even attend college. The experiment had worked so well that Sandy had started a group called Support Dogs for the Handicapped so that others could benefit from having a dog like hers.

I was thrilled! Here were the "friends" that could give an invaluable helping hand—or paw—to handicapped or disabled people. And here was the challenge I had been looking for. I picked up the phone and called Sandy. I'd start a group of my own in St. Louis!

With Sandy's long-distance encouragement and advice, I actually was able to train Max to pick up objects, to prop open doors, to carry the phone receiver to and from its cradle, and to help me get in and out of my wheelchair.

Soon I was speaking to local groups and organizations, explaining how useful support dogs could be. If I could arouse interest and raise money for a nonprofit organization in the St. Louis area, then I could educate others and help train dogs for handicapped people who might not otherwise know about or be able to afford training a dog on their own.

People listened sympathetically—but found it hard to understand how such a program would work in a *practical* way. My words weren't enough. I needed a dog right up there with me to demonstrate.

I tried to use Max. But Max didn't like crowds and would freeze or retreat into the wings.

I *had* to have another dog. I talked to breeders, went to dog shows, answered ads in the paper. I saw sleek dogs, fuzzy dogs, well-bred dogs, frisky dogs—all handsome and well-groomed. But they were too high-strung, or too skittery, or too lackadaisical. No, not one animal I "interviewed" seemed right. But somehow I sensed that God had a dog waiting for me out there—a special dog.

And then one day while I was visiting the Open Door Animal Sanctuary in House Springs, about twenty miles from my home, I passed the pen where puppies were kept.

And there sitting stoically among the bouncing, rollicking pups, was a huge mound of a grown-up dog, with large, dark eyes and a penetrating gaze.

At first I almost laughed out loud. On my second look, I almost wept. I can't remember seeing a more road-worn, tattered animal. The dog was scarred and bruised, but his big brown eyes seemed to be telling me something.

"What are you doing here with the puppies?" I asked. His tail gave a thump. As I walked away, I knew he was watching me.

"That's Jocko," the girl in the office told me. "Or at least that's what we're calling him." He'd been found wandering on the highway. He was part Great Dane, part retriever, around four years old and probably had been abused. "We had to put him in with the puppies," the girl explained, "because he kept jumping our fences, and the puppies' pen is the only one that's covered."

I walked back to the pen. On closer inspection, poor Jocko looked not better, but *worse*. An infection had eaten away part of one ear. And when, with an apologetic air, he leaned back to scratch, I saw that his paw pads were raw.

He was a mess. Who would ever think of adopting such a dog?

God would. *Look beyond the outward appearance*, a voice inside me whispered. *This dog is special. This is the one you've been looking for.*

I took Jocko for a "test run," walking along the road. He wasn't spooked by roaring cars or sudden noises or new people, and he seemed alert and easygoing.

When I took him home, the rest of the family was aghast.

"That's the new dog?"

"Gosh, he's a mess."

"Support dog? He doesn't look like he could support himself."

And then my husband drove up, took one look out the car window, and drove off in mock horror. After circling the block, he returned, and got out to gape. "You've got to be kidding," he said.

But Jocko didn't seem at all concerned that he wasn't getting the "Beautiful Pet of the Year" award. He wagged his tail, and by the next day all I heard was, "We're keeping that nice dog, aren't we?"

I scrubbed him up, gave him his medicine, and just two days later took him to a muscular dystrophy camp. Jocko quickly became the center of attention, and loved it. He didn't cringe or snap when eager-but-uncoordinated hands reached out to pet or hug him. And if it was awkward for a person in a wheelchair to reach him, he would maneuver his head under that hand. Ah, this was the temperament I had been searching for.

Now how would he take to training? Well, he didn't have to be taught to be a ham. On Halloween he went trick-or-treating, carrying a purse in his mouth and acting as if he had done it all his life.

But what about the specifics and disciplines of training? I started by teaching him simple commands like "come," "stay," "heel," "sit" and "stand," using both voice and hand signals. I helped things along by hooking Jocko's leash to Max's collar; when Max performed his own retrieval tasks, Jocko was pulled right along.

The weeks went by. Jocko had to be trained not just to pick up an object, but also to hold on until a hand was ready to take it. Picking up a telephone receiver was one thing—but if the receiver was dropped halfway across the room, it didn't do a handicapped person much good. Over and over and over again I worked with Jocko, sometimes assisted by Max, until Jocko got the point: Pick up an object and carry it to the waiting person's hand.

Nine months passed. Jocko's appearance underwent a startling transformation. His emaciated frame filled out, his coat started to shine. His once-infected cauliflower ear was still scrunched in, but now he stood tall and had a spring in his step.

Jocko was ready for his first demonstration. I took him before a group of rambunctious second-graders. As Jocko retrieved a pencil, an eraser and assorted other objects, the youngsters watched in rapt attention. And they burst into applause when Jocko helped me out of a chair by pulling me up as I hung on to his leash. Jocko's performance was flawless; I said a silent prayer of thanks. This *was* the special dog God had intended for me.

Soon Jocko and I were doing two to four demonstrations a week. He would pick up my cane, my keys—even a dime. He would help me up steps, or stand still and firm so that I could show how someone who had fallen could use a dog as a brace to get up.

By now people were asking for "the lady with the big yellow dog." Jocko had become a pro, ready and willing to be petted, talked to and photographed.

Over the following months, more and more people were able to *see* how helpful—even essential—a dog could be to a handicapped person.

Bit by bit, people offered money, time, skills and services. In May 1983, Support Dogs for the Handicapped was officially incorporated in St. Louis as a nonprofit organization. And Jocko's stardom continued to grow when he was nominated as Service Dog of the Year. But in spite of his newfound fame, he still kept all four feet on the ground: Whenever I had a relapse and my back acted up again, Jocko still acted as my support dog. He literally gave me a boost and eased my way.

Again and again Jocko rose to the occasion. And because of him, a whole new battalion of dogs and a lot of puppies are doing the same. Today, in addition to the adult dogs that our group trains, we also breed the most suitable dogs and will start training puppies at the earliest possible age.

I think back to eight years ago. A raggedy old pooch and a frustrated former invalid—both of us needing something to do. And I thank God, who got us together and turned us into a golden dog and an active lady, eager to let you know that, no matter how bent over or beat up you are, you too can rise to the occasion. And have the full, rich life God intends you to have.

You can bet a pen full of puppies on it.

A Horse Called Amber

Mary D. Wilson

This is a story of two horses, one a jet-black mare called Midnight—some would call her a "devil horse"—and the other, my favorite, a gentle six-year-old palomino called Amber.

Shortly after my husband, John, had bought Midnight, I went out to work with her. I led her out, locked the stable door behind me, and proceeded to saddle and mount her. Midnight was nervous. She skittered. Within seconds she became violent. She reared and threw me to the ground, then went berserk, rushing wildly about the yard. Suddenly she headed back to me at full gallop, teeth bared. Already in great pain from a shattered neck joint, unable to move, I knew she was trying to kill me, to stomp me to death. "Lord, Lord," I screamed, but there was no one near to hear.

No one human, that is. Unbelievably, Amber came charging out of the stable. She hurled herself at Midnight, savaging her with her teeth. Midnight retreated, charged again, retreated again and came back again. Amber stood her ground, defending me until Midnight gave up.

And to think that I'd last seen Amber in her stall, a restraining chain across its entrance. And the stable door—it was locked. I myself had carefully slipped the metal bolt.

Yet my gentle Amber had rescued me. She had overcome the barriers between me and her. Had done that with crucial and uncanny speed.

How?

5

Mothering

Mother to Mother

Gynnie Trautvetter

$\mathcal{I}$ used to be one of those fretful mothers, constantly fearful of what might happen to my three children as they began venturing out into this dangerous world of ours. Then one spring morning in the year that Randy, my oldest, was in kindergarten, an unexpected visitor came knocking at our farmhouse door.

Thump, thu-u-mp.

The yellow school bus had just disappeared down the road and I had started to wash the breakfast dishes when the sound came again: *thump, thum-u-mp.* Insistently.

I looked out into the breezeway. A small bird was fluttering against the storm door, its beak pecking determinedly against the glass. It was a little sparrow and it was obvious by now that it was trying to get inside.

I opened the door and instantly, full of purpose, the bird flew into the loft over the summer kitchen. Moments later it was back, wanting out. It didn't take me long to figure that my little sparrow had some hatchlings (only a mother could be so persistent!) in the loft. *But how did they get there?* I wondered, and then I remembered that earlier in the year a blustery wind had blown the breezeway storm door against the house, crashing out one of the panes. Not until planting season was over had we found the time to replace the glass. In those weeks my mother sparrow must have made her nest in the summer kitchen loft.

From then on I became this determined little sparrow's doorkeeper. I opened the door each time she wanted in or out, marveling at how she seemed to assume that I would always be there to help. Gradually I found myself identifying with her, mother to mother. I felt as though I was God's instrument in helping the sparrow, almost as if He had appointed me.

Though I yearned to see how the mother sparrow's babies were getting along, I never went near them, not wanting to risk disturbing them unduly. But how curious I was! One morning, however, I heard the sparrow's morning "call" and opened the breezeway door for her. But instead of immediately flying off as she usually did, she flew to the edge of the loft and perched beside three of the cutest, fluffiest, plumpest little creatures I'd ever seen. "At last!" I exclaimed, beaming at her. "And you want to show off your children to me, don't you? Well, they're beautiful!"

Still the mother didn't move. What did she want? "Ahh," I said, "it's time to teach them to fly, right?" I pulled a chair over to the wall, climbed up and held my forefinger as a perch for the nearest baby. It hopped onto my finger as though it was the most natural thing in the world to do. I teetered down off the chair and went outside.

It took only a moment for the baby bird to gather the courage to fly, a little awkwardly, into a poplar in the yard. I returned to the others, which were patiently waiting. I repeated the process two more times. Then I held the breezeway door open for the mother. But she didn't move.

"Do you want to talk?" I asked her, half seriously. "Well," I told her, "we did it. Your three young 'uns are on the road to independence, and they're going to be fine. You can be proud of them—and yourself too."

Still she sat there. Again, something told me to climb up on the chair and put out my finger. She hopped right on.

I went out the door with her, talking all the way. "You're such a little thing," I said. "I'm glad you let me help." She seemed to listen, cocking her head as if she understood every word. Out in the yard, she sat looking directly into my eyes. I had the curious feeling that she was thanking me. *I trusted you and you did not let me down*, she seemed to be saying. And in that moment I began to think: If I was truly God's instrument in looking after this mother sparrow and her hatchlings, wouldn't God see to it that I and my children were looked after too? I knew that from that moment on I would not be a fretful mother. The next time Randy boarded the yellow school bus, I would be a trusting one.

For a moment longer the mother sparrow lingered on my finger, then she flew away.

FLEDGLINGS

They were teetering bravely
  On the birdbath's brink,
Two small new sparrows
  Learning how to drink.

Two small fat sparrows
  With feathers all awry
Must have brought a twinkle
  To the Father's eye.

—— *Jane Merchant*

A NICHE OF SERENITY

Isabel Champ

Last spring our newspaper printed an unusual photograph of a downtown traffic light. There right inside one of the three cuplike openings was a tiny robin's nest.

This traffic light hung high above one of the busiest intersections in the city. It certainly was not a quiet spot. Horns blared, brakes screeched, and trucks emitted sooty diesel smoke and fumes.

Yet there inside the nest, built right against the bright red light that flashed off and on, day and night, three little fledglings peacefully slept and fed. In the midst of all the noise and clamor, Mother Robin had established a niche of serenity for her family.

My mother did something similar for me. Early in their married life my parents did not have a great deal of security, and there were ups and downs. But had my mother waited for ideal conditions in which to raise a family, I would not be here today. And yet I have carried the fruit of her transforming love and devotion within me all my life. It has sustained me in times of sorrow and blessed me in times of joy. My mother's quiet strength and steadfast faith are a priceless legacy to me.

EASTER AND AN IMPERFECT WORLD
Elizabeth Sherrill

*I*t had been a long trip, leaving home after Christmas, getting back now a week after Easter. We'd been in Singapore, on the equator, where there is no spring. And upon returning home there were no clues to the resurrection season here in our house either.

"It's almost as though Easter never happened this year," I moped to my husband, John, as we pulled soiled clothing from our suitcases. I was having my usual case of post-trip letdown. I carried an armload of clothes to the basement. There was no sense in getting out the Easter decorations now. "But at least," I called upstairs, "let's take that dried-out old Christmas wreath off the door!"

All of a sudden John came bounding down the stairs. "Come with me!" he said. "Out the back door!"

Silently he led me around to the front of the house. A small brown house finch and her red-headed mate scolded from a maple as we tiptoed to the door. Among the browning hemlock twigs of the Christmas wreath a tidy round nest held three speckled eggs.

All three have hatched now: three down-covered chicks many times the size of those tiny eggs. How was so much peeping energy and eagerness ever enclosed in those confining shells? How did a tomb ever contain the Lord of Life Himself?

Of course, we haven't been able to use our front door since getting home— and we're getting a little tired of those basement stairs. But they're a small price to pay for the greatest Easter decoration we've ever had.

I've learned something else from that finch family. The mother's flutterings remind me of myself when our own three were young.

There's a deeper parallel, though. Raising a family, at the outset, probably didn't seem an especially terrifying prospect to this drab little bird. She and her handsome mate, after all, had found a nesting site far removed from ugliness and danger, a snug private world in which to bring up the children.

The truth about that world turned out to be very different. The isolated haven was revealed—on our return from a trip—to be the front porch of a busy household. Unthinkable monsters shared her children's very neighborhood.

As a mother of the Vietnam era, I sympathize with this small, nervous bird. Who had heard, when we built our nest here in Westchester County, New York, in the 1950s, of drugs in the quiet suburbs, student strikes in the high school? The birds aren't giving up, of course. Parents don't. But they're teaching me a secret about living in an imperfect world. Whenever they can snatch a moment from their anxious labors, the finches sing.

THE EAGLE
Barnabas M. Ahern

I shall never forget the day that I stood in Jordan, on the barren plain at Petra with its walls of blood-red rock. Glancing up, I saw a large bird soar from a mountain crag. Something dropped from its back like a stone. In a moment the stone unfolded, and I saw a little bird stretching its wings to fly. Before long, however, the uprush of wind proved too strong and the little bird, once more a stone in the sky, began to drop. In an instant the mother bird swooped down and caught it on her back to bear it aloft for a second trial. This time the young bird sustained itself longer in flight; but once more it crumpled before the wind and began to drop. But the ever-present mother saved it again for a third testing. As before, the baby eagle dropped, the wings opened, but this time the young bird flew off into the distance in the security of its mother's shadow.

As I watched, fascinated, I recalled the biblical description of Yahweh: "As an eagle incites its nestlings forth by hovering over its brood, so He spread His wings to receive them and bore them up on His pinions" (Deuteronomy 32:11, Douay).

SQUEAKY AND HER PIGLETS
Carol A. Virgil

Carrying a five-gallon pail of pig feed in each hand is burden enough. But I had a load on my mind, too. As I plodded heavily toward the pigpens east of the grove, an angry scene from earlier in the day kept running through my head.

My three daughters had been leaving for school and, as usual, six-year-old Milne had mislaid her mittens. "Why can't you keep your stuff together?" I'd yelled at her. "We have to go through this every morning!"

"I just *had* them," Milne said, nearly in tears and overcome with frustration.

I scurried around, one eye on the approaching school bus, and finally found an extra pair of mittens—dirty and a size too small, but they'd have to do. I thrust them at Milne and shooed all three girls out the door. The picture of little Milne pulling on the scruffy mittens, her head down, lagging behind her two sisters, lingered in my mind as I rounded the corner of the barn with the buckets of pig feed.

Pigs have a built-in timer that goes off at mealtime, and a mob of them was pressed up against the fence like fans waiting for a rock star. As soon as they caught sight of me, they began squealing and oinking and jumping on top of one another trying to be the first at the food.

With a mighty throw, I pitched the contents of the first bucket onto the feeding floor while half a dozen hungry sows converged on it snooting and snorting. With a second throw the other bucket was empty. Instantly the only noise to be heard was moist, avid munching. I was about to turn away when a different sound registered—the high-pitched squeals of newborn piglets.

Baby pigs are supposed to be born in the barn, where it is nice and warm, not outside in the cold. These squeals were definitely coming from the three-sided shelter in the east pen. I stared into it hoping my ears had deceived me. But no, there was a sow on her side and several little heads bobbing up and down.

As I started to climb over the fence, I seemed to remember my husband, Lyle, saying that some sows in this pen would need to be moved to the barn sooner or later. Sooner would have been more appropriate!

I made my way to the shelter to inspect the situation. The new mother and her farrow of six were nestled in the back trying to keep warm. But with the temperature at 10 degrees above and a windchill factor well below zero it was a hard task—especially for those little ones.

"Squeaky!" I mourned to the pig. "Your timing *could* have been better!"

We're not in the habit of naming our pigs except when some personality trait sets one apart from the rest. Like Steeplechaser, who could leap high fences in a single bound. Or Houdini, the great escape artist, or Jezebel, whose behavior would have put the original bearer of that name to shame! But this girl was a different sort, kind of easygoing, and she had a peculiar squeak when she moved her jaw a certain way. So we had dubbed her Squeaky. Now here she lay out in the cold, right in the middle of farrowing.

I decided that the piglets would have to be moved down to the barn to keep warm. When Lyle came home, we could move Squeaky too. But first I had to finish the chores and get things ready in the barn. Quickly I fed the rest of the pigs, found a heat lamp and made a pen for the babies, thinking all the while, *Why don't these things happen when Lyle's home?* Then I made my way back up the hill, back over the fence and back into the shelter. Things were not quite the same.

"You've been busy while I've been away," I said to Squeaky. Two additional wet little pigs were bumping around, trying to find something to eat. Two new pigs. That should make eight.

"One,two,three,four,five,six,seven . . ." I was never very good at math, but I knew Squeaky had had six piglets before, and that these two were new. That should make eight, but I could find only seven. I was pretty sure I knew where number eight was. Under Squeaky.

Squeaky had changed positions while I was away and that eighth piglet hadn't moved fast enough to avoid being rolled on. It happens a lot, even under controlled circumstances, but out here in a pen with other sows and the cold it was even more likely. I knew I'd have to hurry if I were to save the rest of the litter.

Just then Squeaky moved slightly. I glimpsed the little one beneath her and quickly pulled it out. Though I was sure the piglet was dead, there might be the slimmest chance. Without much hope, I started to hit the little pig gently on the side. Was that a heartbeat? I slapped it, pounded it, shook it. All of a sudden it took a gasping breath of air. I hadn't really expected any results, but now I felt like Florence Nightingale, Angel of Mercy! Maybe I could bring this little guy around.

Determined now to save the piglet, I sat down on the cold ground and tried to make myself comfortable. I laid it in my lap, wrapping my coat around it. As I patted and stroked, the piglet took more breaths. Minute by minute, it actually came alive in my hands. And as I sat there luring life back into the little pig, something odd happened.

My thoughts began to seesaw back and forth between the little pig in my lap and the picture of Milne walking dejectedly to the bus. What was the connection? I hadn't physically hurt Milne, as Squeaky had her offspring. On the other hand, I *had* hurt Milne emotionally. And over such a small thing. After all, losing mittens is just part of being a six-year-old—not really important enough to make a big deal over. A small grin found its way to the corners of my mouth when I thought of all the times I'd set down something or other and couldn't remember where I put it.

Apparently my motherly instinct hadn't been working too well.

"Squeaky," I said to the old sow, "I crushed Milne's spirit this morning just as surely as you steamrollered this little one in my lap."

With a jolt, it occurred to me that God was using the creatures I loved least in the world—pigs!—to show me a shortcoming in my own life. It wasn't the first time He'd done this, either.

"Why pigs, Lord?" I whined. "That's hard on the ego. Couldn't You use a more socially acceptable creature—like a lovely doe or a beautiful German shepherd—maybe even a white woolly Columbia ewe?"

I guess I shouldn't have whined to Him, because immediately my mind began to dwell on the virtues of the sows who are really good mothers. How carefully they lie down so as not to hurt their young by accident. How they instinctively lift their feet higher to avoid stepping on the little ones. I hung my head. "Okay, Lord, if pigs can be that sensitive, then I can certainly try to be more careful in the future to protect my girls' fragile self-images."

Very early the next morning, Milne came creeping into Lyle's and my bedroom. It was still dark, but the glow from the security light in the barn-yard illuminated the chilly room just enough for me to make out her features.

"I woke up, Mom," she said, rubbing her sleepy eyes. I was about to say the usual—"Go back to bed, it'll be morning soon"—when I remembered certain events of the day before.

"Why don't you crawl in here?" I said, pulling back the blankets. And just as I'd seen a piglet out in the cold respond to me, I now saw a wispy smile steal across Milne's face, making her small nose crinkle up in its own peculiar way. Then a twinkle jumped into her big brown eyes as she climbed in beside me.

As I watched Milne drift off to sleep—safe, contented and loved—I thanked God for caring enough to show me things in my life that I need to work on, "Even if You do have to use pigs to make Your point."

A LOVING TEST

Arthur Gordon

The other day, sitting quietly on our little dock that overlooks a tidal creek, I saw a mother raccoon lead her three babies out of the tall grass on the far side of the creek and onto a fallen tree that stretched out to deep water. She dove in gracefully and swam around, chirring at the little ones, coaxing them to join her. They just looked dismayed; obviously they had never tried to swim. This was to be their first lesson.

The mother climbed back up on the tree, took one baby in her mouth and swam across the creek with it. She did the same with the second. The third waited expectantly for his free ride, but nothing happened. The mother called to him from the far bank; she didn't go back to him. He grew increasingly agitated, crying piteously and dipping one timid paw into the tide. The mother's answering calls became fainter. She was leaving him—or so she seemed to want him to think.

Finally, with a desperate plunge, the baby threw himself into the creek and floundered frantically to shore, where I was sure that in a minute or two he would brag to his siblings about how brave he was.

An analogy? I think so. That raccoon mother chose the toughest of her babies for her little lesson in loving. She tested him because she knew he could respond. She seemed to abandon him, but she never did.

6

Grieving

The Mockingbird's Song

Mary Lou Stribling

For months my mother had been ill. As I watched her grow weaker, I wondered, is this all there is? You live a good life, then die. Just that?

Over and over, as I sat by her sickbed, I read to her from the Bible, "The Lord is my shepherd. . . ." She knew it by heart but never tired of hearing it read aloud.

One night, after an especially bad day, Mother lifted her head and looked toward the window as if she listened for something.

"What is it?" I asked.

"He'd better hurry if he's going to sing again," she said.

My sister-in-law and I drew close to her, puzzled. Then she smiled at us. "It's just a bit of foolishness," she said, "but there's a little bird out there. When the pain is bad at night and everybody is asleep, he comes and sings to me."

My sister-in-law and I looked at each other and shrugged. It was the drugs we decided, a form of hallucination.

A few nights later we knew that the end was very near. I walked outside in the cool October air, trying not to think beyond the pale square of her lighted window. Suddenly from above me there came a burst of song so pure and perfect that it hit my ears like an electric shock. There were trills almost too high to hear, low throaty croons as tender as a mother comforting a restless child. Was this, I wondered, the bird that Mother knew?

The mockingbird sang on without pause. And as I listened, there in the darkness, somehow the words of the Twenty-third Psalm came into my mind. "Yea, though I walk through the valley of the shadow of death. . . ."

At that moment, after all those readings, for the first time I realized that the word in the psalm was *through* the valley, not *in*. The valley was but a phase of the journey, not a destination.

By morning, the bird was gone and so was Mother. Now, after months of strain, I was at peace. But I knew that the bird's song would be heard again—and that Mother would emerge from that valley into a place where singing never ends.

SINGING IN THE RAIN

Laura Kohr

A deep hush was in the church; only the soft voice of the minister could be heard. Outside the windows slanted the gentle rain. Inside, the air was heavy with the perfume of flowers. My heart was leaden and my body was numb. It is never quite possible to be ready for separations. My husband was gone; only his body remained. I listened to the minister's words, trying to find comfort.

Then, incredibly, it happened. Far away through the rain I heard the robin's song. He sang through the rain, despite the rain. He put his whole small heart into that song, and a voice within me repeated his message just as clearly as if it had been spoken in words: "Do not grieve; there will be happiness and song for both of you, beyond the tears."

All at once the crushing burden seemed lighter. A moment later when the congregation sang the final hymn, I found that I could raise my heart to my Creator in song, just as the robin had done.

Later, when I spoke of this to others, no one else had heard the robin sing. Perhaps I dreamed it, I don't know. It doesn't matter. I can hear it still, whenever I need the faith and courage to go on.

A Song on a Bare Bough

I saw a valiant cardinal
Dark-red against the winter dawn,
He whistled from a leafless tree
Upon a barren lawn.

The tiny dauntless splotch of red
Shot up a challenge straight and high:
A rocket-burst of silver stars
To shower a winter sky.

The little brave intrepid thing:
A conqueror of cold and night.
He drenched the bare boughs suddenly
With color and with light.

A triumph and a victory
That I have come to understand.
I laughed—a broken laugh—and took
Life once more by the hand.

— *Grace Noll Crowell*

Winter Prophecy

Faith is like the cardinal—
Among trees silvered thick with ice
   Against the snowing;
I heard his call exulting twice
   Of spring
And green buds blowing.

— *Catherine Cate Coblentz*

THE NIGHT THE DOG HOWLED

Elizabeth Gunn

A dog howled throughout the night that my husband, Dudley, died, an eerie background to the prayers of our minister and the sobbing of myself and my three daughters. Now a year later, another dog was howling.

I had not known why the dog howled that night Dudley died—an odd coincidence perhaps—but this night I knew the dog and why he was howling. He was a once beautiful German shepherd named Roy, now chained shelterless to my neighbor's garage door.

I got out of bed and started for the medicine cabinet. No, I must not. I had already taken more pills than I should. I looked down into the yard from the upstairs window. The two blue spruce trees had been white with snow that night, too, and all the houses had been dark at two in the morning, the time it was now.

I knew what my daughters, my friends and minister were saying about me. "She is going to lose her mind if she does not stop wrapping herself in her grief."

I went down the hall to the back bedroom window. From here I could see the small, neglected-looking house next door that belonged to a man named Tom. The dog looked like a thin gray ghost. He stood, head down, crouched against the garage for protection against the wind and falling snow. His long nose pointed toward the full moon as he howled.

Maybe if I give him something to eat, he'll stop, I thought irritably. I put on shoes and a warm robe and went downstairs to find a bone.

He leaped toward me, straining at his chain. Then he grabbed at the bone. His teeth went deep into my hand. I stood there, seeing my blood, red against the white snow.

Then the strangest thing happened. That hungry dog dropped the bone. He began licking my hand, still red with blood. His brown eyes were as full of penitence and distress as a human's could be. A light went on in my neighbor's house.

"Is anything wrong, Mrs. Gunn? What are you doing out there?"

"Feeding your dog, Tom, to keep him from howling. He has just bitten me."

"I'll be right out."

In a minute Tom and his wife, hastily dressed, were beside me. "Oh, Mrs. Gunn, it's a bad bite. We're so sorry."

Tom's wife put her arm around me, brought a towel for me to wrap around my hand. "We must get you to the hospital," she said.

The dog still crouched, the bone untouched, his eyes never leaving my face. I stooped down and with a stick pushed the bone toward him. "Eat it, Roy. It's O.K. You didn't know what you were doing."

He took the bone eagerly.

"He has turned crazy since his owner died," Tom said. "The owner's son gave him to me, but I'm going to take him to the dog pound."

"No," I said, getting into their car. "Give him to me."

They looked at me as if they thought I was crazier than the dog. But I was not.

For the first time since Dudley's death the darkness in my heart had been penetrated by a light. I saw hands being held out to me, just as my hand had been held out to the starving dog. I saw the big, long-fingered hands of our minister, the hands of my daughters, the manicured hands of my friends. Loving hands that my self-pity had made me reject just as the hungry dog had thought in that first minute only of his own need.

I was not crazy. I was simply saving myself by saving Roy. For I had suddenly learned that the way out of crippled grief is to find another cripple and help him—even a dog.

Roy is a sleek 120-pounder now—a friendly, loyal animal. There will always be a scar on my hand just as in my heart, but both hand and heart are functional, and the scars grow dimmer with the years.

Until Healing Comes

Mary E. Mauron

Mourning was always a strange word to me—full of images of thick black veils, dirgelike music and faces blank with forced-march resignation. When our twelve-year-old, Lawrence, died in a boating accident, our family was plunged into that world of mourning, and I was suddenly living out those images. I *felt* that thick black veil covering my bleeding heart. There was a dirge too—the unanswered questions, the pain-filled memories that kept the wound open. Though I had tried to walk hand-in-hand with God for many years, it was often agonizing effort and sometimes only pure decision that kept me going on my own forced march for my family's sake.

Perhaps the questions were the hardest part of that march. There was the day the whole family brought a garden gift to the cemetery. While my husband, Ray, and our other children searched for water for the plants, six-year-old Kris and I sat waiting by the graveside. I was holding tears in check, busily brushing grass clippings off the simple stone marker when I felt a tug on my coat. "Momma, was Lawrence in that big box they put under the ground here?" I drew my son to me and rocked him in an embrace. Tears spilled over as I desperately looked to Heaven for a wise way to explain, but nothing came to light.

"Where are You, God?" I cried inside. "Help me understand, or how can I ever help these little ones?"

That night I haltingly attempted an explanation as I snuggled Kris in bed. Three others crept in to listen and ask more hard questions. "I don't get it, Mom. When God saw the boat was in trouble, why didn't He do something?" "Why did God want Lawrence with Him now?" "Am I going to die before I grow up?"

Memories, too, were so hard. There was the day that eleven-year-old Paul dug out Lawrence's trademark, his coonskin cap, to wear while riding his newly inherited bike. Seeing the flash of bike and hat going down the driveway opened the dike yet one more time. The same thing would happen when Lawrence's good friend Raelyn (who is also his sister) frequently played the tape from his last school concert. Pride and pain accompanied each flashback of Lawrence's first—and last—drum solo. Together our family avoided the silent drum set, his mitt and special blue aluminum bat and his penny collection. We had decided to set aside his "treasures" until we could decide when and how best to share them. Each question, each memory hurt so!

Weeks turned into months as I struggled through the alternatives of stoic resignation, emotional indulgence and intellectual comprehension. They were all dead ends. Then, in a remarkable way, God showed me *His* simple truth.

The healing lesson began the day my son discovered our family cat on his bed, a swelling we had noticed on his forehead now an open wound. Together we got Tiger wrapped in a towel and to the vet, who diagnosed a deep abcess, probably resulting from a bite in a cat fight. The wound closed over on the outside, but kept festering underneath.

As the vet explained the seriousness of Tiger's condition and the need for antibiotic treatment and surgery, I stood washed again with the pain so easily triggered since the accident. Why this poor animal? Why this additional suffering?

Though my silent cries of "Why, God? Why more now?" were usually followed by "Thy will be done," it was said more with resignation than conviction.

That theme was repeated often through the next weeks as we tried to help Tiger recover. The vet gave instructions to open the wound daily and apply antibiotic powder each time until the healing progressed from the inside out. Each day was a painful trauma as someone had to catch the cat, wrap and hold him in a towel while another "operated."

After two weeks I called the vet to vent my utter frustration. "It's not getting any better. How can a wound heal if you open it every day?" The vet calmly reminded me that we were not just opening the wound, but were adding a healing antibiotic powder to it each time. He said there was no quicker way to heal an abcess that deep. We were to continue the procedure until we could see healing taking place inside to out. I hung up and cried, for I simply did not believe him.

It was another week before some slight improvement seemed to be taking place. And it was at this point I learned that one of my neighbors was moving. She was a woman who had continued to say "I am sorry your son is dead" by frequently sending over gifts from her garden and kitchen, though she had never called or come over herself.

I had not written any acknowledgement cards yet, so I thought I would walk across the street to thank Mrs. Burge before she moved. She met me at the door and invited me in with a sad smile. Tiny worry lines were etched over a face that somehow seemed much older than her fifty-odd years. We sat over tea as she apologized for never coming over after our tragedy, explaining how hard it was for her to face that particular kind of pain.

"You see," she said as she stared at the cup and saucer on her lap, "twenty years ago we lost . . . our only child when she was just . . . thirteen and . . ." A sob escaped her throat as she covered her face with her hands. I reached for her cup and set it on the table while struggling to free my own heart and voice. I searched for a way to respond that would not add to her hurt. For a few moments two broken-hearted mothers just sat wordlessly with each other. I did try to reach out to her with words of God's ultimate trustability, but I did not seem able to comfort her. I left with a heavy heart.

Taking the long way home, I pondered it all again. Wearily I asked God if my broken heart could ever be whole again. Then suddenly, dazzlingly, the whole situation of the cat's deep wound and slow recovery flashed before my mind. Surely, surely, that was it! For twenty years Mrs. Burge had had a festering wound—opened frequently, but evidently not filled each time with a healing substance that would have allowed healing from the inside out.

It was like the sun shining through after a hard rain, for now I knew I had a choice after all. Over the coming years the choice will not be whether to open the wound of Lawrence's tragic accident and death. That will often be beyond my power as other people or situations inevitably call forth the memory. Rather, the choice will be each time to invite and allow God's healing love to fill the open wound—submerging and washing the unanswered questions and raw edges of pain in the balm of His wisdom, His comfort, His healing wholeness.

Yes, the day came when we did not need to wrap the cat, open the wound and apply the healing powder. Tiger's skin finally drew together in complete wholeness. I, too, am recognizing—almost two years after our tragedy—an inner pulling together into wholeness, a little more after each time of applying God's healing love. I am recognizing His special kind of healing taking place in me—from the inside out.

BIRDNESS

Jake, who'd fallen crippled
From my tree,
Was especially dear
To me.
I watched him
Stumble, mutter,
Day on day,
Whether in wind or away from it,
Flitter, flutter,
Fume and sputter.

He kept trying;
I spied him regularly
Struggling up unseen
Steps into the sky—
Mumbling, fumbling,
Day on day,
Flittering, fluttering,
Fuming, sputtering . . .

Then away!

I cannot remember whether
It was a propitious
Windy day or not;
Only that,
Lured by the beyond,
And some beyondness in him
Jake had flown,
And now roams elsewhere.

So may I, birdlike,
Seek beyond—
To painful impediment inured.
The sky is mine,
Knowing
That
Flight is in the bird.

— Sallie Chesham

7
Loving

LOUIE, THE TOUCHER

Glenn Kittler

Recently I attended a large cultural gathering of mostly strangers. I saw people greeting one another with smiles and handshakes, hugs and kisses and an occasional touch to an arm or a pat on the back.

I probably wouldn't have given it a thought except that I heard a woman nearby say, "Have you noticed how people are always touching each other?"

The woman with her said, "Yes, I have. Why do you ask?"

"I don't like it," the first woman said. "Somehow it just seems like an empty gesture. It's meaningless."

Then I thought of Louie. People unfamiliar with the ways of cats may not believe this but my cat Louie is a real toucher. He was about a month old when he moved in with me. Once he discovered where at home I work and spend most of my day, he decided to join me, curling up under the desk and resting his head on my foot. When I get up and move about, Louie follows me and when I go back to my desk, he curls up again and puts his head back on top of my foot.

This has been going on now for ten years. No matter where I happen to be in the apartment, Louie is there, too, touching me with a paw or brushing against me. I don't know whether he does this to let me know he is there or to be sure I am here, but I do know that I like it. And it gently tells me I'm wanted and needed.

No, a touch isn't an empty or meaningless gesture, it's a silent way of letting the heart say what really doesn't need to be said.

AND THEN, ALONG CAME TOBY

Lois Allen Skaggs

At our house, in 1981, we had a problem that seemed almost hopeless. Cleo, my husband, had suffered two severe heart attacks and now, unable to work, he had taken to drinking. It was a familiar cycle: a period of sobriety, then a drinking bout, followed by remorse and another stretch of sobriety. Sometimes in those drying-out periods, I'd find him sitting on the edge of our bed, staring at the floor. The humiliation in his face—his sad brown eyes—would speak for him. "I hate myself. Just look what I'm doing to myself. I should be taking care of you."

Many times I'd think I couldn't go through it again. I'd cry out to God, "Oh, help this man who is so unhappy with himself. Help me, I don't know what to do. Please, please, take over."

And then, along came Toby. A kitten. My daughter Ann was in the process of moving to her own apartment, and Toby started out as her pet. "Mom," she said one day, "I bought a little Siamese cat. Can I bring him here till I move? Just for a few weeks?"

Inwardly I groaned. To me, pet spelled p-e-s-t. But what could I say? Ann had already bought him. "Okay," I said reluctantly. "But only till you move."

"Thanks, Mom." She grinned. "Oh, you'll love him, wait and see."

"I doubt that."

But, as I discovered, Toby was hard to dislike. He had limpid blue eyes—even tiny eyelashes. His fawn-colored coat was soft and shiny, long for a Siamese; his ears, paws and "mask" a deep dark chocolate brown. He was the washingest kitty I'd ever seen. Lying in the sun on our back porch, he'd lick one little brown paw with his tongue and scrub his ear again and again, then do the other one.

I'd always heard that Siamese were likely to be aloof. Not this one. He actually seemed to cultivate us and seek affection. Especially from Cleo.

Shortly before her moving day, Ann got some bad news. "I can't take Toby with me, Mom. The landlord says 'no pets.' I guess I'll see if my friend Tammy can take him to her family's farm."

Cleo and I talked it over. When Ann moved, Toby stayed.

We let him come and go as he wanted. Soon I could open the back screen door, yell "Toby!" and he'd come running as fast as he could fly, his paws barely touching the ground. He ran after birds, butterflies. On his first excursion up our walnut tree, he got stuck. When it began to rain, we had to ask our neighbor Ron, who owns a tall ladder, to rescue him.

Before long, Toby established routines with Cleo and me. In the morning, he'd hop up on our bed, settle down between us, and purr us awake. When I came home from my job as a switchboard operator on the evening shift at Farmington Community Hospital, Toby met me at the back door—as if to remind me that he'd been doing *his* job of keeping Cleo company while I was gone. It was a job he took very seriously.

He played with Cleo constantly, and when Cleo took a nap, Toby curled up at the foot of the bed to take a nap, too. If Cleo watched television, Toby climbed into his lap. He followed Cleo everywhere. When Cleo worked in the yard, Toby had to inspect everything that was done. Cleo even asked his opinion.

"How's that, boy? Think that will do?"

"_____"

"Yeah, I think so, too."

When Cleo walked across the driveway to sit with Ron on his porch steps for a neighborly chat, Toby would follow and lie between his feet, patiently waiting. After the visit, Cleo would say, "Well, Toby, let's be on our way," and off they'd go, Toby trailing behind.

Watching, smiling to myself, I'd think, *I do believe that cat thinks he's a dog.*

One evening Cleo was sitting in his favorite chair, a recliner, leaning back with his hands clasped behind his head. Toby jumped onto the table by the chair and meowed, looking intently at Cleo.

"What do you want, Toby?" Cleo said.

"Meow."

"What do you want, boy?"

"*Meow, meow,*" Toby cried, louder. Taking his hands down, Cleo leaned forward. "Toby, I don't know what you want!"

Toby promptly sprang up and stretched out full length along the top of the backrest. That was *his* favorite spot on Cleo's favorite chair.

When he told me about it later, Cleo said, "That boy can talk. He was telling me to move my arms out of the way."

Toby was telling Cleo something else, too. Something we didn't recognize till later.

After breakfast one morning, Toby went to the back door, meowed and sat down. That meant he wanted out. Cleo opened the door, but Toby just sat still and looked up at him.

"Well, go on out, if you want, boy." Cleo nudged him lightly, so out he went.

An hour or so later, someone knocked at the front door. Cleo went to answer. I heard a man's voice. "Do you own a Siamese cat?"

"Yes, we do," Cleo replied.

"You'd better come with me," the man said.

I dropped to my knees. "Oh, no, Lord. Please, no!"

Cleo came in through the back door, his chin trembling so he could hardly get the words out. "Toby's been hit! Honey, he's dead."

"Oh, Cleo!"

"He's lying on the back porch. The man said he just couldn't help it. Toby jumped in front of the truck. He wasn't mangled, he looks like he's sleeping."

Cleo choked out the next words. "He loved me!"

"I know, honey."

"He loved me just the way I am."

"I know."

For a while, we didn't speak. Then I put my arms around him. "You know, Cleo, that's the way God loves you, too. Just like you are. His love is just like Toby's, only more. His love follows you, too."

We stood silently, holding each other, for a minute. Then Cleo went down to the basement and found an old tin breadbox and some soft cloth to line it with. He took it out to the back porch. I stayed inside. I didn't want to see Toby. I wanted to remember him alive.

From the window, I watched Cleo carry the box and a shovel down to the back of the garden where he and Toby had spent so much time together. He dug a tiny grave under the peach tree.

I bowed my head. "Lord, is it wrong to love a cat that much?"

The answer came gently, firmly, into my mind: *Through that cat, your husband has been able to feel My love. I sent Toby.*

"Oh, yes, Lord. Thank You."

I peeped out the window again. Cleo was just sitting on the ground, holding the shovel, his head bowed. He sat there a long time, telling Toby good-bye.

From that time on the binges stopped. Cleo began going to church with me. No more than a month later—over two years ago, just before Christmas—he committed his life to Christ. As for me, I'm still learning every day that God's ways are "past finding out." He loves us so generously. So forgivingly. He can even use a little cat to show us that.

Editor's note: A few weeks after Toby died, Ann telephoned to say she'd bought Lois and Cleo another Siamese kitten. "No more pets!" was their reaction. But Ann brought him over, "just for a visit." They named him Tony, "a happy reminder," Lois says, "of the blessing we had in Toby."

A FAITHFUL FRIEND

He asks but little, just a kindly word,
A gentle pat can fill him with real bliss,
Or, humbly, just to lie close to your feet
And sometimes touch your hand with gentle kiss.

If you are feeling sad, he is sad, too,
And gives you sweet condolence with his eyes.
Your presence is the dearest thing he knows,
You are the sun that's shining in his skies.

A little dog so faithfully can be
Your truest friend, he really understands
Your every mood and shows his boundless love
So eagerly obeying your commands.

Horizons go no farther than your face,
To him you are the stars and moon above.
He'll follow you to any distant place,
His eyes shine with a deep, unchanging love.

No matter who you are or what you do,
Your dog remains a true, devoted friend.
He'll share your life, though hungry, poor or cold,
And kiss your hand, quite faithful to the end.

— *Ruth B. Field*

THE THREE OF US

Edda Christine Drey

Smokey was Pete's dog.

From the first days when she came to us as a pup, this Australian blue heeler followed my husband all over our small Iowa farm, trotting happily at his heels while he fed the stock, repaired the machinery and tended the crops. While Pete waved and yelled, Smokey nipped at the heels of our cows and pigs, sorting them out and herding them back to their proper stalls in the barn.

Smokey had Pete's schedule down so exactly that if Pete took a little longer than Smokey thought necessary, she'd bark at him to hurry up. And at night, while we watched television, Smokey would flop at the side of Pete's chair. Granted every now and then Smokey would come to take a sniff at what *I* was up to, but basically that dog made it clear that her world revolved around Pete.

Or so I thought until one unforgettable Tuesday.

On the morning of November 5, 1985, Pete and Smokey set off across the yard, together as usual. Today we were hauling in the corn.

Pete went out on the tractor to do the harvesting. I bumped along behind him on our old H-Farmall tractor, transporting the loads of corn back to the building site beside the hog and cattle yards, where I unloaded them all into the "elevator" that clickety-clacked its way up into the corn crib.

I had already collected two wagon-loads from Pete and was unloading the third, when I realized that some of the ears of corn had spilled onto the ground. As I bent down alongside the moving elevator to pick up the wayward ears, my foot slipped into a rut made by the tractor wheel after a recent rain.

I was trying to regain my balance when I felt a hard tug on my pant leg. *What's that?* I wondered. In a split second I knew.

I screamed in horror and pain.

My coveralls had been caught in the churning power-takeoff that drove the elevator. Within seconds my entire leg had been wound in too.

Somehow I was able to throw myself against the machinery's motor and shut it off. My head and shoulders hit the ground with a thud.

I inched myself up on my elbows and stared up in disbelief at the sight of my foot and leg mangled in the machinery. Waves of nausea swept through me. *I mustn't lose consciousness*, I told myself. *I might never wake up.*

I sank back down and closed my eyes, too sickened to think clearly. In the distance I heard Pete's tractor making its rounds in the fields; my cries would never be heard over the roar. How long would it take before Pete realized something was wrong?

A shadow fell across my face. Smokey. She was standing over me whimpering.

"Go get Pete," I ordered her. "Smokey, *go get Pete.*"

She looked as though she understood what I was saying. She walked a few feet away and started to bark in the direction of the field, then turned and came right back.

I repeated the command. "Go get Pete!"

Again Smokey went a little way and barked in Pete's direction. But she would not go out into the field and get him. Instead she came back to where I was lying and placed her head on my shoulder.

The noise of Pete's tractor came closer. I reached for my cap that had tumbled off, raised my arm as high as I could and waved and waved. But the grass around me was too high. The tractor roared off in the opposite direction.

"Go get Pete!" I pleaded once again to Smokey, and again she got up, went a few feet, barked, and then returned to lie beside me.

I squinted up into the sun. How could this have happened to me? Where was God? Where was God when my foot slipped?

Pete doesn't know why he came to check on me. I'd been helping him with the corn for over thirty years, so there was no reason for him to think I'd need his help. But "for some strange reason" (which is how he put it later) he stopped his tractor and came to see how I was doing.

He found me, still conscious, with Smokey's head on my shoulder.

The following weeks in the hospital were hard. My leg had to be amputated just above the knee. And I had to start readjusting to a new life, with only one leg. Before the accident I'd thought my faith in God had been pretty strong, but now I had to confess there were moments I felt abandoned. Where *was* God when my foot slipped into that rut?

Doctors fitted me with an artificial leg that I strapped around my waist. Getting used to it wasn't easy, but finally I was ready to return home. A bed was set up for me in the downstairs dining room, where I could sit by the window and look out at the neighboring farms. My husband, children and friends were there continually to comfort and help me in all my waking hours. But there were still periods of time when I was—and felt—very alone. What would I do when my family and friends had to get back to their daily routines? Would I be left all alone?

But guess who *never* left my side. Smokey.

I'd never seen such a change in an animal. Smokey parked herself by my bed and stayed there. At night I'd wake up and there she'd be, her head on the covers looking straight at me. She wouldn't even leave the room to eat;

she lost weight and started getting weak, so we had to bring food in to her!

When visitors came and I'd start to get tired, Smokey would put herself between me and them, and bark. She seemed to know exactly how I was feeling at any given moment. And no matter how much activity there was around my bed, she never got underfoot. Although she was known for being pretty lively, she never raced around or got agitated. Pete was afraid she might trip me when I got up. But whenever I tried to walk by myself, using crutches and balancing on my new leg, Smokey moved out of the way. One day when I fell, she ran to the door and barked furiously until Pete came to help me up.

"That dog has set herself up as your guardian angel," Pete said one night after doing the evening chores.

"Some guardian angel!" I sputtered. "Why wouldn't she help me the day of the accident?"

"I think she helped more than you're willing to admit," Pete said on his way to the shower. "She stood by you."

Stood by me.

I stirred uncomfortably on the bed, and Smokey sat up and put her face on the covers. For the first time since coming back from the hospital, I studied her face. I really *looked* at her. There was no mistaking it: In her eyes was a concern that I had been too preoccupied and upset to notice before.

Smokey rested her head on the top of my bed, and I let the love from those eyes flow through me. I almost felt that if she could talk she would have said, "Chris, I love you and care about you. Every minute that you were out there suffering, I was suffering with you."

Then suddenly it was as if God Himself was speaking to me. It wasn't God's fault that I'd been in too much of a hurry to shut off the machinery motor before bending down close to it. The accident was just that, an *accident*. Now through Smokey's eyes I felt that God was trying to say He too had suffered along with me during those agonizing first hours, and throughout the recovery time that followed. They'd both stood by me.

I reached out and rubbed Smokey behind the ears, and her tail began to thump against the covers.

From that point on, my recovery progressed so well that soon I was ready for another leg. It looks so real that I feel comfortable wearing dresses again. Today I drive the car or pickup by myself. I work regularly at the school library and continue to be active in our church. I do all my own housework, and I still help out as much as possible with the farm chores, but I'm mighty careful whenever I'm around any equipment.

Smokey and I are still fast friends. She leaves me now from time to time, but checks with me first. I have to tell her, "You go ahead. I'll be fine." Then she follows Pete across the yard as he goes to do the chores, always looking back to make sure I'm really okay.

Smokey, our Australian blue heeler. Heeler . . . healer? Maybe to some people it's a strange play on words. But somehow I'm sure God used that Australian blue heeler . . . to heal me.

FEATHERED FRIEND

Jo Coudert

I'm going nuts here by myself," Pat Myers confessed to her daughter, Annie. Pat had been virtually confined to her house for a year as she was treated for an inflamed artery in her temple that affected her vision and stamina.

A widow with two married children, she'd been happily running a chain of dress shops. But now that she had to give up her business, her home began to feel oppressively silent and empty. Finally she admitted to Annie how lonely she was.

"Do you think I should advertise for someone to live with me?"

"That's such a gamble," Annie said. "How about a pet?"

"I haven't the strength to walk a dog," Pat said. "I'm allergic to cats, and fish don't have a whole lot to say."

"Birds do," said her daughter. "Why not get a parrot?" And so it began.

Pat and Annie visited a breeder of African Greys and were shown two little featherless creatures huddled together for warmth. Pat was doubtful, but Annie persuaded her to put a deposit down on the bird with the bright eyes. When he was three months old and feathered out, he was delivered to his new owner, who named him Casey.

A few weeks later Pat told Annie, "I didn't realize I talked so much. Casey's picking up all kinds of words."

"I told you." Her daughter smiled at the sound of pleasure in Pat's voice.

The first sentence Casey learned was "Where's my glasses?" followed by "Where's my purse?" Whenever Pat began scanning tabletops and opening drawers, Casey chanted, "Where's my glasses? Where's my purse?" When she returned from an errand, he'd greet her with, "Holy smokes, it's cold out there," in a perfect imitation of her voice.

Casey disliked being caged, so Pat often let him roam the house. "What fun it is to have him," she told Annie. "It makes the whole place feel better."

"I think *you're* beginning to feel better too," said Annie.

"Well, he gives me four or five laughs a day—they say laughter's good for you."

Once a plumber came to repair a leak under the kitchen sink. In the den, Casey cracked seeds in his cage and eyed the plumber through the open door. Suddenly the parrot broke the silence, reciting, "One potato, two potato, three potato, four . . ."

"What?" asked the plumber.

"Don't poo on the rug," Casey ordered, in Pat's voice.

The plumber pushed himself out from under the sink and marched to the living room. "If you're going to play games, lady, you can just get yourself another plumber." Pat looked at him blankly. The plumber hesitated. "That was you, wasn't it?"

Pat smiled. "What was me?"

"One potato, two potato—and don't poo on the rug."

"Oh, dear," said Pat. "Let me introduce you to Casey."

Casey saw them coming. "What's going on around here?" he said.

At that moment Pat sneezed. Casey immediately mimicked the sneeze, added a couple of Pat's coughs at her allergic worst and finished with Pat's version of "Wow!" The plumber shook his head slowly and crawled back under the sink.

One morning while Pat was reading the paper, the phone rang. She picked it up and got a dial tone. The next morning it rang again, and again she got a dial tone. The third morning she realized what was going on: Casey had learned to mimic the phone faultlessly.

Once, as Pat opened a soda can at the kitchen table, Casey waddled over and snatched at the can. It toppled, sending a cascade of cola onto her lap and the floor. "*#@!" Pat said. Casey eyed her. "Forget you heard that," she ordered. "I didn't say it. I never say it. And I wouldn't have now if I hadn't just mopped the floor." Casey kept his beak shut.

Later a real-estate agent arrived to go over some business. She and Pat were deep in discussion when Casey screamed from the den, "*#@!"

Both women acted as though they'd heard nothing.

Liking the sibilance, Casey tried it again. "*#@!" he said. And again. "*#@! *#@! *#@!"

Caught between humiliation and amusement, Pat put her hand on her guest's arm. "Helen, it's sweet of you to pretend, but I know you haven't suddenly gone deaf." They both broke up laughing.

"Oh, you bad bird," Pat scolded after the agent left. "She's going to think I go around all day saying four-letter words."

"What a mess," Casey said.

"You're darned right," Pat told him.

Casey's favorite perch in the kitchen was the faucet in the sink; his favorite occupation, trying to remove the washer at the end of it. Once, to tease him, Pat sprinkled a handful of water over him. Casey ceased his attack on the washer and swiveled his head to look at her sharply. "What's the matter with you?" he demanded.

If he left the kitchen and Pat heard him say "Oh, you bad bird!" she knew to come running. Casey was either pecking at her dining room chairs or the wallpaper in the foyer.

"Is it worth it?" her son, Bill, asked, looking at the damaged front hall.

"Give me a choice between a perfect, lonely house and a tacky, happy one," said Pat, "and I'll take the tacky one any day."

But Pat did decide to have Casey's sharp claws clipped. To trim them without getting bitten, the vet wrapped Casey tightly in a towel, turned him on his back and handed him to an assistant to hold while he went to work. A helpless Casey looked at Pat and said piteously, "Oh, the poor baby."

Pat often wondered if Casey knew what he was saying. Sometimes the statements were so appropriate she couldn't be sure. Like the time a guest had lingered on and on talking in the doorway and Casey finally called out impatiently, "Night, night."

Yet, whenever Pat wanted to teach him something, Casey could be maddening. Once she carried him to the living room and settled in an easy chair as Casey sidled up her arm and nestled his head against her chest. Pat dusted the tips of her fingers over his velvet-gray feathers and scarlet tail. "I love you," she said. "Can you say, 'I love you, Pat Myers?' "

Casey cocked an eye at her. "I live on Mallard View," he said.

"I know where you live, funny bird. Tell me you love me."

"Funny bird."

Another time Pat was trying to teach Casey "Jingle Bell Rock" before her children and grandchildren arrived for Christmas dinner. "It'll be your contribution," she told him.

"Where's my glasses?"

"Never mind that. Just listen to me sing." But as Pat sang "Jingle bell, jingle bell, jingle bell rock" and danced around the kitchen, Casey simply looked at her.

Finally Pat gave up. And all through Christmas dinner Casey was silent. When it came time for dessert, Pat extinguished the lights and touched a match to the plum pudding. As the brandy blazed up, with impeccable timing Casey burst into "Jingle bell, jingle bell, jingle bell rock!"

Pat's health improved so much she decided to go on a three-week vacation. "You'll be all right," she told Casey. "You can stay with Annie and the kids."

The day her mother was due back, Annie returned Casey to the apartment so he'd be there when Pat got home from the airport.

"Hi, Casey!" Pat called as she unlocked the door. There was no answer. "Holy smokes, it's cold out there!" she said. More silence. Pat dropped her coat and hurried into the den. Casey glared at her.

"Hey, aren't you glad to see me?" The bird moved to the far side of the cage. "Come on, don't be angry," Pat said. She opened the door of the cage and held out her hand. Casey dropped to the bottom of the cage and huddled there.

In the morning Pat tried again. Casey refused to speak. Later that day he consented to climb on her wrist and be carried to the living room. When she sat down, he shifted uneasily and seemed about to fly away. "Please, Casey," Pat pleaded, "I know I was away a long time, but you've got to forgive me."

Casey took a few tentative steps up her arm, then moved back to her knee. "Were you afraid I was never going to come back?" she said softly. "I would never do that."

Casey cocked his head and slowly moved up her arm. Pat crooked her elbow, and Casey nestled against her. Pat stroked his head, smoothing his feathers with her forefinger. Finally Casey spoke.

"I love you, Pat Myers," he said.

Part Two

CARING FOR GOD'S CREATURES

8

Overcoming Fear

LITTLE DOG FOUND

Aletha Jane Lindstrom

I saw her first in mid-December during one of Michigan's cruelest winters. She was running across the frozen barnyard, a small ghost of a dog, almost obliterated from sight by swirling snow.

Living in the country, we've become accustomed to seeing abandoned dogs and cats. We seldom see the same one twice, but this one was strangely different. My husband, Andy, and I glimpsed her frequently—in the barnyard, the fields, the woods, along the road. And she was running, always running, head held high, either trying desperately to find someone or fleeing in abject terror.

My heart went out to the small creature. How could she possibly survive the bitter cold? Even Collie, our big farm dog, who loves winter, was content to remain indoors.

But the plight of the little lost dog provided only brief distraction from the black mood that engulfed me. My dad had died recently and it had been hard to let him go. Though I was sustained by God's promise that we'll be reunited with our loved ones, lately there had been dark times when my faith flickered. Could I trust God's promise? The question gnawed at me. For a while I prayed about it, then stopped.

On one below-zero evening, as I walked down the drive for the newspaper,

I sensed I was being followed. I looked back, and there was the lost dog—a small beagle with big freckled feet, a wagging tail and soft, pleading eyes. I removed my mitten, but before I could touch her, she cowered and drew back. Then she panicked and fled to the woods, leaving bloody footprints in the snow.

I couldn't sleep that night; the memory of those eyes haunted me. Had she been stolen for hunting and later abandoned? Where was she now? Had she found shelter from the bitter cold, or was she still running, terrified and alone?

The next morning we followed tracks in the woods until we found her. Andy held out a piece of meat and she crept toward it on her belly. When she drew close enough, I grabbed her. She struggled and cried until her strength was gone. Then she lay whimpering in my arms.

We wrapped her in a blanket and took her to the vet. "Poor little mutt," I said as we carried her in. "He'll probably have to put her down."

The vet removed the blanket, now bloodstained, and ran gentle, capable hands over the emaciated body. The head, it seemed, was permanently tipped to one side. She was covered with cuts, welts and scars, and the pads were worn from her feet. "She's either been running for days over frozen ground or digging to make a bed in the leaves—probably both," he said.

Silently we awaited the verdict. "She's a good little beagle," he said at last. "I think we can save her."

"Then I'd better advertise for the owner," I said.

"I wouldn't bother," the vet replied. "She's smart. If she's from around here, she'd have found her way home—that is, if she'd wanted to go . . ."

"But she's so frightened. How long before she'll get over that?"

"Never—not entirely. Apparently she's been badly abused. When that happens, a dog becomes either vicious or afraid for the rest of its life." His voice softened. "And obviously this little dog will never be vicious."

"You mean she'll even be afraid of us?"

"Probably." He was silent for a moment and then added thoughtfully, "But we can't be sure. Sometimes love works wonders."

That night I brought a dog bed from the attic and placed it near the kitchen stove. To my surprise she crept in immediately, settled down with a long sigh and closed her eyes. For the first time the trembling stopped.

I knelt beside her, my mind filled with questions. This small stranger, seemingly from nowhere—why had she approached me in the drive, pleading for affection? And why, needing it so much, had she fled in terror when I offered it? It seemed we had something in common. We were both afraid to trust.

Gently I stroked the soft ears. "You can trust us, Puppy," I whispered. "You needn't be afraid—ever again." I placed an old shawl over her and tucked it in, making sure it would stay.

"It seems we have ourselves another dog," Andy said the next morning.

I nodded. "I'm not sure I'm happy about it. Now that Tim's away from home, I figured we wouldn't get another dog . . . after Collie. They all die and break your heart sooner or later." *That's the way with love*, I thought, remembering Dad.

"Let's forget the heartaches," Andy said gently, "and remember the happy times. They've given us so many of them."

He was right, of course. I couldn't imagine life without a dog. Besides, I'd already succumbed to this one. She was so hurt and frightened, so little and alone. And she needed us so desperately. Her eyes, her most endearing feature, were dark puddles, reflecting her emotions. I longed to see them shining with eagerness and love—as a little dog's eyes should be.

We continued calling her "Puppy." Somehow it seemed to fit. I remembered what the vet said about her fear, but I couldn't believe she'd be afraid of us. She was. She allowed us to minister to her injuries, but when we reached out to pet her, she cringed and pulled away, as if she feared we would strike her. I wondered if perhaps that was why her head was tipped.

We gave up trying to pet her. "She'll come to us when she's ready to trust us," I said. But the rejection hurt. I wondered if that's the way God feels about us when we fail to trust Him.

Andy, unaware of my thoughts, said, "She'll learn. It's a beagle's nature to be happy and affectionate."

"Love casteth out fear," I said, quoting 1 John 4:18. Here was another of God's promises. Could I believe this one?

Weeks passed and Puppy didn't respond. Collie seemed to be her only security. I usually walked Collie down the lane in late afternoon. When Puppy's paws were healed, she joined us. Sometimes she'd wander off, following a scent. But when she discovered she was alone, she'd race back to Collie.

Those were the good days. There were other, heartbreaking ones when the beagle seemed to be in a trance. She'd wander to the roadside and huddle there, a solitary figure, gazing up and down. I'd send Collie to bring her back. Inside she took to her bed, her eyes confused and unseeing. I'd sit by her and slip my hand under her chin. "Is there someone you love, Puppy? Someone you've been searching for?"

At such times I wished I knew where she'd come from, what she'd experienced. Then, looking at the sad eyes, the ugly scars, I decided I'd rather not know.

By late spring I noticed changes in her behavior. Her trips to the roadside grew fewer, and she waited as impatiently as Collie for our walks. There were times, too, when we were petting Collie, that she'd draw close and watch wistfully. And that was the way things remained.

Then one September afternoon I leaned on the back fence, watching our two dogs. They were in the far side of a back field engaged in a recently discovered pastime, chasing grasshoppers. Collie hunted with her eyes, leaping on her prey. Puppy hunted with her nose, snuffling along the ground. Only her waving white-tipped tail was visible above the weeds.

I watched in amusement. The little dog had been with us eight months now, but she was still afraid, still wouldn't come to be petted. Despite our hopes, our prayers, love hadn't worked its magic after all. Yet just having the small dog and knowing she was enjoying life lent pleasure to my days.

Collie saw me and came running. I knelt and put my arms around her, my eyes still on the waving white-tipped tail moving in the maze of weeds. Suddenly Puppy discovered she was alone. She darted in frantic circles until she caught Collie's scent. Then she came racing toward us.

When she reached us, she pushed her eager, squirming body between Collie and me. She looked up, her eyes shining with that soft light that comes only from the heart. "Me too!" they plainly said. "Love me too!"

"I do love you, Puppy. I'll always love you," I said, snuggling her close. So love *had* cast out fear, just as the promise says. "It's all right, Dad," I whispered. A gladness was rising in me that I hadn't felt for a long time. I knew then that God is faithful to *all* His promises.

THE BLACK SHADOW

Samantha McGarrity

For nearly three years a huge black German shepherd roamed our neighborhood, until one day I brought him home. Despite his ferocious appearance, George, as I later named him, was extremely shy and it took me the next two years to convince him that no one wished him harm.

He was a gentle dog, loved and admired by everyone in the community, and eventually he became very docile and obedient. He took up the back seat of my VW whenever I went on trips or shopping forays. He loped along behind my bicycle, plunged into the Croton River with me in the summers, paddled behind when I went canoeing or rowing, took hikes with me, from his corner in the kitchen watched me cook . . . and invariably ended up in the center of things whenever I gave a party or invited friends in for dinner.

I guess you could say that George was like my shadow. He had needed someone to love him and care for him. Now that he belonged to someone, he had found his purpose in life—that of being *my* dog and *my* companion.

Now whenever I look at my contented canine friend, I find reflected in his eyes the same security I find within myself when I turn to *my* Lord and Master. And I would know then that just as George's days of loneliness and seeking are past, so are mine!

HEALING FROM TERROR

Diane Komp

Ashley—a pre-owned Yorkie from the Humane Society—came into my home with his head hung low. The neighbors were all waiting for me at home to meet the newest member of my family. That was when we learned that this little dog was terrified of men.

In their presence, Ashley would shake like a leaf. All my men friends are gentle, but their imposing sizes and booming voices seemed to terrorize him. I had to find a way for Ashley to be healed of his fear!

Whenever a male visitor came to the door, I would pick up Ashley and hold him in my arms. I would ask my friend to pet the dog gently and talk to him in a soothing voice. When the little guy relaxed, I would hand him over to my friend to hold and continue petting for a few more minutes.

After some weeks, Ashley seemed to remember each man he met in this way, and stopped cowering and shaking in their presence. In fact, after meeting my next door neighbor Bob, Ashley stole into his house, then reappeared a few minutes later to drop one of Bob's dirty socks at his feet. Bob, he seemed to be saying, was not only safe, he was accepted!

Since coming into my family, Ashley has been healed of his fear and to this day lives at peace with all men. It's the love he's been getting that's healed his fear—I'm sure of it. And not only is Ashley a beloved family member now, but he reminds me how to approach all the abused and fearful people I meet. The best way is to start with love.

'Fraidy Cat—Jessica

Marion Bond West

My five-year-old cat Jessica was terrified of the vacuum cleaner from the time she was a kitten. Often the vacuum and I would surprise her by entering a room where she was sleeping. Instantly her eyes would flash open, her ears flatten in fear and she would dart out of the room in panic.

One day as I took out the vacuum, I spoke to her in my most gentle, reassuring voice: "It's all right, Jess. Trust me. You're okay. Stay put, kitty." The usual terror filled her eyes, and her ears flattened back, but she remained curled up on the bed as I vacuumed around it. This happened again . . . and then again. Finally the day came when she would open one sleepy eye, glance at the vacuum in ho-hum fashion and continue her nap.

I learned something from Jessica. You can't outrun fear. Sometimes you just have to stand your ground. Jessica ran for five long years but now she can claim victory over her mortal enemy, the vacuum cleaner. Like Jessica, I'm learning to heed that Voice that comes to reassure me when something frightening looms on the horizon of my life and I am tempted to flee in panic. Standing fast is difficult at times, but when the victory comes—as it surely will—what joy and peace we have won!

'Fraidy Cat—Minnie

Marion Bond West

Fear was creeping up on me as I sat in my living room. I needed to confront a neighbor who I felt had slighted me, and as I tried to pray about it, confusion mounted and my prayer felt empty. Suddenly, our new stray cat Minnie jumped on my lap. It took me a moment to realize that she was fearful. She stood almost paralyzed, staring at something with her ears flattened and her eyes widened.

Finally, I located the source of her fear. Minnie had seen my china cat sitting under a table. The statue looked quite lifelike. I picked it up to let my cat see that it wasn't real. She immediately buried her head under my arm and refused to look. I stroked her and talked to her and gradually she lifted her head, still clinging to my arm. Ever so slowly Minnie sniffed the large china cat. Then she cautiously placed one of her paws on the statue's pink nose. She looked at me in astonishment and then with pleasure. She began to purr. I put the china cat back under the table, and Minnie hopped down and sauntered over to sniff it once more . . . maybe even to become friends.

Watching her walk confidently around the statue I thought, *Father, I do believe You can teach me about fear and trust, even from a cat!*

I went to the door. I would call on my neighbor and reach out past my fear. And with His help, maybe even find the way to restored friendship.

9

Doing the Loving Thing

LETTING LOUIE KNOW
Glenn Kittler

When I was a new cat owner, I read a newspaper article claiming that household pets, especially those that did not go outdoors, adjusted to the routines of their owners. Any sudden change of routine on the part of the owner could cause the animal to become upset or withdrawn. Working at home as I do, I thought that I spent plenty of time with my pet. But during some weeks my schedule was irregular and my cat would grow unusually quiet and distant. The article stated that when this kind of reaction occurred, the owner should explain the situation to the animal. Although the pet would not understand, at least it would not feel abandoned. I followed the article's advice—and it worked!

Late one afternoon I was preparing to leave my apartment with a visitor. I went over to my cat, who was perched on his favorite chair. "Now, Louie," I said, bending down to his level, "Mr. Davidson and I are going out for something to eat. You have everything you need, so you take care of the apartment and I'll be back around ten o'clock and I'll tell you all about it."

"What in the world are you doing?" my friend gasped. I told him about the newspaper article. He asked, "And that works?"

I nodded.

Halfway through dinner my friend said, "I've been thinking about you and your cat. Wouldn't it be nice if people communicated with one another like that? There would be less hurt, less argument, less pouting, less misunderstanding." I thoroughly agreed with him.

When I arrived home that night, Louie was waiting for me just inside the door. He arched his back and rubbed against my legs, purring all the while. I began to tell him about my evening. Yes indeed, my friend was right. Would that we humans could learn the art of communicating with one another. Love and understanding would surely follow.

CAPTAIN'S QUILT
Sue Monk Kidd

Not long ago our old springer spaniel, Captain Marvel, had to have surgery. When I left him at the vet's, he looked at me with big, sad eyes. Back home I glanced at his quilt nestled on the carpet. He'd curled up on that old lap quilt day and night for years. It was where we knelt to scratch his ears and where he retreated after his baths. Remembering his sad look, I had a thought. *Carry Captain the quilt.* But it seemed like such a silly idea. Drive all the way back just to take a dog a quilt . . . the vet would think I'd lost my grip. Besides, I was very busy.

But Captain had washed the children's faces with sloppy kisses, pulled their wagon and chased their sticks for eleven years. I picked up the quilt and drove back to the vet.

I felt awkward handing it to the receptionist. But she smiled. (I think she'd seen my type before.) She left, then reappeared a moment later. "Poor dog's been crying all morning," she said. "But when I slipped the quilt in his pen, he curled right up on it and closed his eyes."

That little quilt had made all the difference. And driving home, I had a new sense of just how important even the smallest gesture of love can be.

FINNEY, THIRSTY—AND LOST
Terry Helwig

From the study window, I saw him: a large black poodle wandering aimlessly, his pink tongue hanging like a limp rag. He plopped down in the shade of a neighbor's tree. Obviously he was tired and thirsty—and lost!

I needed to water my flowers anyway, so I went outside, turned on the hose and whistled. The black head jerked up. In an instant, the poodle was waist-high beside me, slurping cool water from the hose. I managed to read his tags. "Is your name Finney?" I asked. His tail wagged.

As I opened the front door, Finney tried to follow. But my cat Buddy hissed his disapproval. "You'd better wait here, while I call your owner," I said.

Getting no answer, I returned and opened the car door. Without hesitation, Finney jumped in. And off we went. Finney recognized the white-frame house of his owner right away; he pranced and yipped.

No one was home, so I fastened him to his long chain in the backyard. "I'll keep calling until I get someone at home," I assured him and patted his curly forehead. As I started to leave, Finney woofed one strong, loud bark. I smiled, looked back into his dark brown eyes and answered, "You're welcome."

Had he really barked me a thank you? Maybe not. But one thing was certain. Helping Finney had brought a bit of sunshine to my soul.

SPARROWS, WORMS
AND LITTLE GIRLS
Dorothy B. Trefry

Mother! Mother! The men are at the school cutting down a great big elm, and in one of the hollow limbs is a bird's nest with three baby birds. They've been hurt and they're hungry. May we bring them home to take care of, please? Please, Mother?"

With many misgivings, I finally yielded.

"We will try, girls, but you must be prepared for the fact that we might not succeed. Baby birds need to be fed constantly; the mother and father birds work steadily all day to keep the hungry mouths fed. You must realize that it is a long, tiresome job, one you cannot neglect. I shall be much too busy with the baby to help you."

"Oh, Mother, we will!" chorused Margaret and Dorothy, with friend Judy chiming in, "I'll help! I'll help!" and off they dashed to the rescue.

Shortly, they came trudging back up the street with their little family. The poor starlings were in a semi-comatose state from the fall and very frightened.

It was a busy afternoon, fixing up the box in the cellar for them to live in and trying to discover something for the wee things to eat. Everything was tried. The girls dug worms, which the birds spit out in disgust, being either too young to take them or needing the mother bird to masticate for them. They settled that day for just giving them drops of water.

It was a long night for me. My older daughter, Margaret, who was to be nine in the fall, had several illnesses behind her, and was inclined to be overly emotional. I kicked myself for giving permission for the venture, feeling that the poor birds would not survive, that this would upset her greatly and that we would have more trying weeks on our hands. Margaret slept like a log; but Dorothy, the carefree six-year-old, tossed and fussed in her sleep. I felt her forehead. It was hot.

"What could be the matter this time?" I murmured as I made my way to bed. We seemed to be plagued by one illness and crisis after another, with scarcely a breathing space in between for a husbanding of resources. Finally I dropped off into a troubled sleep.

Next morning at dawn the birds were chirping for food even more insistently. Dorothy awoke hot and uncomfortable—it was mumps. With a heavy heart I started my day, trying to send my husband off to his work with a smile. How was I going to manage?

"Take it slow, Mother," I cautioned myself, "one step at a time."

First, I called the doctor, then went to Margaret who was already fretting about what the poor little birds were going to eat. Judy was at the back door waiting for my daughters to come out. I sent her home, saying that we had mumps, but Judy was back in a flash, saying blithely, "I've had them! Now what will we feed the birds?"

I looked in the cupboard and saw a can of dog food. "Here, girls, try this," I said in desperation. I thought that this impossible task would keep them busy for a while but, strange to say, the birds loved the dog food.

From that day on the birds thrived and grew. They were fed every hour, on the hour, and two more faithful parents three birds never had. For two weeks, while Dorothy struggled with the mumps, they bathed the birds, fed them, cleaned out the nest, scared away dogs and cats, washed their own hands, and then repeated the whole routine over and over again.

Dorothy developed mumps meningitis and for five days knew nothing. Consciousness would come to her occasionally and she would ask for the birds: "Make them stay, Mummy, 'till I get better . . ."

Stay they did, every day growing stronger, healthier and more tame. Soon they needed feeding only four times a day, leaving the little mothers time for play. It was quite a sight to look out of the window from my vigil by the sickbed and see two little girls playing paper dolls with the birds perched upon their shoulders or strutting around their feet.

Indeed, it was a comforting sight to me. *His eye is on the sparrow . . .* kept running through my mind. I could not place where I had heard or read the phrase, but during the many days of Dorothy's convalescence, I thumbed through my Bible often, until finally I found these words in Matthew 10:29: "Are not two sparrows sold for a penny? And not one of them will fall to the ground without your Father's will. But even the hairs of your head are all numbered."

And I understood. Our Father knows and cares what becomes of us.

The day finally arrived when Dorothy could make the big journey out to the yard. The birds were soon foraging for themselves, but they continued to play with the girls and in the evening would come down to the back door for their dog food.

Today, though our birds have long since flown, the message of courage they brought is still with us—the courage that comes from a knowledge that God is with us always.

SANCTUARY

Ralph Heath

When my assistant, Mary, stuck her head into my office to report that Rick Johnson had shown up to work, I threw down my pencil. "Oh, no!" I snapped. "Tell him we don't need anybody."

This wasn't true; we always need someone to help with the care and feeding of sick and crippled birds in our Suncoast Seabird Sanctuary. But Rick Johnson was one creature not welcome here.

Two years earlier we had accepted him to fulfill a court sentence of forty hours of community service by doing carpentry work in the sanctuary. He had been charged with drunk driving. Then, with ten hours left to work, he came to me on the afternoon before his final court appearance.

"Could you sign those ten hours off for me?" he begged. "I'll come back and finish them up next week, honest."

Something told me not to do it, but those dark brown eyes looked so pleading. And I knew he'd be in real trouble if I didn't. So I signed.

That was the last I saw of Rick Johnson—until now.

I wanted to go out and tell him off. Not only did he cheat us, the court and the state of Florida, but he also had put us under a fearful responsibility.

"Tell him to go away," I said, turning back to my work.

"He says he wants to work seventy hours," said Mary.

"Seventy?" I looked up. "He only owes us ten."

"Yes, but he says the Bible told him to work seventy."

The Bible? I had to go out and see this man. The Bible is very important to me. The Lord helped us get this sanctuary started twenty years before, and He had saved it from disaster time and again. For instance, hurricanes somehow just went around us.

But what would a phony like Rick Johnson have to do with the Bible?

I found him looking up at our pelican roost. "You know," he said, "I could expand it to make enough room for twice as many birds."

"What's this about seventy hours?" I asked. "Not that we'd want you around here, anyway."

"Well," he said, pulling at his chin, "I'm sorry for what I did, Mr. Heath. I've become a Christian. I was reading my Bible the other day, and in Proverbs it says that if you cheat someone, you have to pay it back sevenfold. So I figure I owe you seven times the ten hours I skipped out on."

I stared at him. A one-legged sea gull laughed raucously and a white egret with a steel pin in his broken wing twisted his head around toward us. What was his game? Maybe he wanted to use our place to keep out of sight.

"I don't know," I said, scratching the back of my neck. "We really don't need any help around here right now."

"Well," he said, looking back up, "I can see where that pelican roost needs some support." The man was persistent, I had to admit.

"No," I shook my head with finality. "We really don't need any help right now."

I turned and walked back to my office, where I busied myself with clinic records and tried to forget Rick Johnson's remorseful brown eyes. It's a lot of work keeping tabs on all the sick or hurt birds we find, or that people bring to us. Some six hundred birds were recuperating in our pens, cages and roosting areas. Most would fly back to normal lives; others would find a comfortable home here.

My door burst open and Mary stuck her head into the room. "Ralph, he's back!"

"Who's back?" I asked, hoping she wasn't referring to Rick Johnson.

"Roman."

"That ornery pelican?" I rose from my chair.

"Yes. I found him waiting at our front gate."

Roman was a brown pelican who had been carried in here two years before. Tangled up in fishing line, with a lure hooked in his big leathery bill, he appeared to be dead. Our doctor snipped off the hook barb, then carefully backed it out of the bill. Then he unwound yards of tough monofilament line sunk deep into the bird's leg.

The brown pelican is an endangered species, and many die tangled in fishermen's lines. Instead of reeling in the ensnared pelicans and trying to help them, anglers often cut the line. Trailing lines can snag in trees, where the birds are trapped and starve to death.

Roman, however, didn't appreciate our ministrations. As I held him for the doctor, he snapped at me with his big bill. I still carry the scar on my arm. He had a bad temper and, even when recuperating, seemed to blame me for his bad luck.

Frankly, I was relieved when, recovered, he flew to the roof of a nearby motel. Then, flapping his big wings, he disappeared over the Gulf.

Now Roman was back again.

"What is it this time?" I asked.

"He has a broken wing. You can see the trail in the sand where he dragged himself up the beach to our place."

Birds often show up at our door when hurt or sick. Many have been previous patients.

I walked into the examining room where Roman lay under the care of one of our technicians. A big yellow eye rolled up at me.

"Hey, old fellow," I said, stroking his pulsing brown neck.

Snap! He tried to bite me. The scoundrel!

I laughed. "That's the way it is with birds," I said to Mary, who stood by. "They react without knowing what they're doing."

"Yes," she said, "just like us. We hurt each other not meaning to. Only difference is," she added, "we're sorry about it later."

I looked at her out of the corner of my eye. "Have you been talking to Rick Johnson?"

"No," she looked startled. "Why?"

"Never mind," I said, helping put the splint on Roman, who looked as if he would be staying with us for some time.

Roman—Rick Johnson, I thought, as I carefully placed the big pelican in his recuperation cage. Broken wings—broken relationships. Are they much different?

I tried to put myself in Rick Johnson's shoes two years earlier. He had been frightened, like the pelican. He didn't mean to hurt us any more than Roman did. But there was a difference. Rick had come back to say he was sorry, and to offer quite a bit more at that. If we could give animals a second chance when they hurt us, why couldn't we do it for humans too?

I walked back to my office and picked up the phone. I had to admit the pelican roost did need some work. Rick Johnson said he'd be in the next day.

I never saw a man work the way he did. Day after day he threw himself into practically reconstructing the sanctuary. He rebuilt the pelican roost, fashioned new perches for the eagles, renovated the cormorant feeding pens. All in all, he made quite a difference.

When his seventy hours were over I hated to see him go. I found him working in the roosting area. "Rick, how would you like to stay with us, work full-time? We need someone like you."

He wheeled, and squeezed the air out of me with a big bear hug. "I was hoping you'd say that!"

That was three years ago and Rick Johnson has been one of the Suncoast Seabird Sanctuary's finest assets. He is an expert carpenter, and the place has bloomed under his hand.

He's also made a friend of Roman, who has become a permanent resident. Rick handles him without fear and Roman doesn't snap at him.

Maybe Roman has learned to give us humans a second chance, too.

THE HELD-UP JOB

Drue Duke

Construction of the house in the block down the street seemed to be progressing nicely. Then—all of a sudden—the work came to an abrupt halt. When I saw the contractor's car in the driveway, I strolled over to inquire.

"Come with me," he said, a twinkle in his eye.

He led me around the house and through the back entrance. There he pointed to the space where the electric fuse box was to be installed. He motioned me to be quiet but to peek into the opening. Inside I saw a small brown-twig nest that held a little bird, its bright, inquisitive eyes fixed on me.

The contractor led me away and spoke in a low voice lest the tiny tenant be disturbed. "We're letting the birds finish their job," he said, "before we go on with ours."

A warm glow enveloped me as I walked home. The contractor's consideration of the little bird was a reminder to me of my God-assigned responsibility to protect all of God's creatures—great and small. An important task—one that I relish sweet reminders of from time to time.

WHITEY

Grace Randall

*A*ugust 14, 1988, was one of the hottest days of a record-breaking heat wave that gripped New York City last summer. I got up early that morning, and the temperature was already inching toward the ninety-degree mark; it would be the thirty-first consecutive day in the nineties, and the humidity was brutal. There seemed to be no end to the misery. A still, steamy haze covered midtown Manhattan, and the air pollution index was reaching a critical point. News reports urged people to take it easy and stay indoors.

I love animals. The first thing I did that morning was tend to my own menagerie: six cats, a yellow-naped Amazon parrot, an injured pigeon I was nursing back to health, a half dozen tropical fish, forty roofbirds and my nineteen-year-old Border collie, Angel. The stairs would have been hard on Angel. So I carried him down the six flights when I took him out. Like so many animals, this dear one couldn't fend for himself without the help of a person.

After feeding and walking my old friend, I went back out to buy some groceries at the corner store. By now the air was suffocating, and I wondered how God felt about all the animals in the city who had no way of escaping the merciless heat, especially the horses who pull tourists in carriages around Central Park. I always pray for animals, as well as people—but I couldn't help wondering sometimes: Is God moved when I pray for animals? There were moments, depressing moments, when I felt that the work I did for various humane societies and animal shelters was for naught.

As I approached Sixty-second Street and Second Avenue I saw an elderly woman holding onto a parking meter and looking as if she were about to be ill. As a nurse, I thought I should see if I could help. But the woman shook her head. "It isn't me," she said, pointing to the corner where a silent crowd had gathered. "It's that poor horse. He's dead." I crossed the street to where a spotted, white carriage horse lay on his side.

The horse wasn't dead, but he was in really bad shape. He was heaving and foaming at the mouth. Several perspiring police officers struggled to hold him down. His big, soft brown eyes were wide with terror. One of the cops attached a hose to a fire hydrant and began soaking down the thrashing creature. *God*, I thought, *please don't let this beautiful animal die like this.*

He was obviously suffering severe heat prostration, and probably vascular collapse (not enough critical fluids circulating through his large body). I knew that if this horse didn't get immediate medical attention he would most likely expire right there. Pushing through the throng, I broke to the front and addressed a patrolman. "I'm a nurse," I said. "Perhaps I can help . . ."

"I don't know what anyone can do for that horse," he sighed, pushing back his cap, "unless someone can get a whole lot of I.V. equipment here real fast."

I.V. equipment. I didn't have anything like that in my apartment, but I knew someone who might. Dr. Patrick Cotter, a veterinarian with the New York Humane Society, lived right around the corner. I raced to the pay phone on the corner and dialed his number. Dr. Cotter answered.

"Grace, I'm bedridden with the flu, but if you can get over here, I'll gather up the equipment you need."

I ran all the way to Dr. Cotter's building. By now the temperature was nearing a hundred. Would the horse be able to hang on till I got back? Running in that heat nearly finished me; it was terrible to imagine how that horse must have felt hauling a carriage through the park.

Dr. Cotter handed me tubes, catheters, and a number of bags filled with electrolyte solution (a fluid containing calcium, potassium and other salts). Grabbing the supplies, I raced back.

The crowd had swelled to several hundred. "Please, let me through," I implored. "Please." More cops had come, and they were restraining the horse while they played the hose on him. But the animal was snorting and fighting, wildly delirious. *How long can his heart stand the strain*, I wondered. *With all these people around him he must be absolutely terrified. He probably doesn't even know we're trying to help.*

A couple of young people stepped forward to lend a hand, veterinary students from Colorado, in the city for vacation. We quickly hooked up the tubes, readying the horse for intravenous infusion. Already on my knees, I leaned over to take a closer look at him.

The poor guy isn't going to make it, I thought. I put a hand on his heaving chest. I could feel the life draining out of him. He'd all but stopped struggling now. His eyes were rolling back in his great, noble head. His breathing was labored, erratic. His gums had turned white from shock, and he was dehydrated. I winced at the nasty, bleeding gashes on his body where he had slammed against the heat-softened tar and gravel of the street; the tar and gravel and blood were beginning to clot the raw wounds. I wanted to turn my head away. Surely this was not the death this wonderful creature deserved, collapsed in a puddle of blood, water, urine and sweat in the middle of a big, boiling city.

"Just hang on!" I whispered in his ear. "I'm praying for you."

I closed my eyes. "God, if ever You answer another one of my prayers, please let this be the one." I kept repeating my prayer, like a chant, as the water from the hose splashed up in my face, soaking my clothes. Then a strange thing happened. A voice came to me, a voice I had never heard with such force and clarity before. It was as if God were speaking directly in my ear. *"Grace, I will let you save the horse."*

I was awed. How could *I* save the horse? I'd done all I could. Now it was up to God. But the message left no room for doubt: *I will let you save the horse.*

Ever since I was a little girl, I've cared for animals. All I knew to do now was to *love this horse back to life.* I buried my face in the moist folds of his powerful neck and stroked his chest. "Don't die," I murmured in his ear. I wanted to make my will for him to live become his will. "Don't be scared. You're safe now. We want to help you. Just don't die. We can save you with our equipment, with our love. You're scared and tired. But hang on. Try. *Fight.* I love you."

I thought again about how hard it must have been for him to haul a carriage through the park. He was not an old horse, but neither was he a young one. "I promise you," I said, "that you will never, ever have to pull another carriage again. I give you my word."

He was becoming weaker in my arms, weaker by the minute. It was so hot. The policemen kept playing the hose over us. Nothing we were doing seemed to be helping. The horse's breathing grew more sporadic. Suddenly it stopped altogether. I could no longer feel his heart hammering against his chest.

No! I thought. Cupping my hands over his nostrils, I took a deep breath and blew into them. It worked on people, why shouldn't it work on a horse? Again and again I forced air through his nose. *Come on. Breathe. Fight!*

With a great snort and a kick of his leg, the horse resumed breathing. He struggled, then his eyes rolled all the way back in his head again. He was just barely hanging on and I wasn't about to let him quit. Two more times he stopped breathing. Both times I got him started again. After the third time he tried to get up, but we eased him back down. He was looking stronger. His eyes were clear and his breathing steady. I sat back. The police attached ropes to him, then we counted off: "One . . . two . . . three! Up you go!"

He wobbled a bit, staggered, but he stayed up! He looked dazed and woozy, but he took a few tentative steps. He shook his head as if to disperse the cobwebs. *He'd made it.* I heard a sudden, tremendous roar. All around, people were cheering wildly. So many had stopped to watch the drama that I couldn't guess the crowd's size. And they had stayed quiet during the three and a half hours we'd worked on the stricken animal. Now from the roofs of buildings, from balconies and open windows, people were yelling and clapping, even crying. I heard the whine of cameras as photographers snapped away. Television news cameramen rolled their tape. It seemed as if, on this sultry day in August amid a brutal heat wave, all New York paused to watch this horse battle for life. We'd fought the battle with him. We'd all taken part in a joyous miracle, a miracle on Sixty-second Street.

Shortly after the horse regained his hooves, a vet from the police department stable arrived. I learned that the horse's name was Whitey. Poor Whitey. We loaded him into a police horse trailer and chauffeured him to a nearby stable, where the vet performed a gastric lavage (pumping fluids directly into his stomach) to flush out Whitey. We also cleaned the wounds he'd sustained those times he struck the pavement. He was in much too critical a state for strong, medicinal solvents to be applied, so we had to use mayonnaise—that's right, jug after jug of mayonnaise, which gently cleansed the damaged tissue without hurting Whitey. For days after, I smelled like a mayo sandwich. Each time I got a whiff of myself I would grin.

That night at the stable I noticed an ashen-faced young man standing off to the side. He was the driver. "I don't care if he ever pulls a carriage again," he whispered, "just so long as he's all right." I smiled in relief. Already the promise I'd made Whitey was coming true.

A few weeks later the New York Bureau of Animal Affairs made it official: Whitey would never be made to pull a carriage again. I visit Whitey every so often on the farm where he's been retired. When last seen he was romping happily alongside the mare and colt who share his pasture.

The day after I helped Whitey, *New York Newsday* ran a front page picture of the scene and described me as an "anonymous good samaritan." I liked that, because the parable from Luke 10 is one of my favorites. "Go and do likewise," Jesus said. That steamy day in Manhattan taught me a lesson. There is mercy for *all* creatures, and prayer *is* heard. There is joy and meaning in treating one another with love and compassion. God blessed me with the chance to go and do likewise. For Whitey.

10

Disciplining for Happiness

THE ART OF DISCIPLINE

Phyllis Hobe

You know how it is—you see a winsome little puppy and it's love at first sight, usually mutual. Then the puppy begins to grow up and get into trouble . . . and you don't know what to do.

"Take him to Obedience School," a friend suggested. I really didn't want to do that. It sounded like a harsh solution and, after all, he *was* only a puppy. But eventually, when I was about to run out of shoes because Trooper had chewed them all to shreds, I gave in. I enrolled both of us in an obedience class.

The group met twice a week. All of us were beginners. And at first we thought we would never get through to our dogs. It took a lot of repetition, endless patience and heaps of praise. But eventually owners and pups began to understand what each expected of the other. We owners were learning to speak with loving authority and our dogs began to take pride in their accomplishments. The whole experience brought owners and pets closer together than ever before.

There is a word for this kind of process and I had never understood it until now. It's *discipline*. Discipline is truly an art. Actually, it's an act of love because it says to the other, "I care about you." Never harsh but always firm, it takes time, wisdom . . . and devotion.

Now I know why God is so patient with me.

GROWING PAINS

Shari Smyth

I look at Roscoe sleeping sweetly in his crate, his paws twitching as he dreams. I wonder what a seven-week-old Labrador retriever pup dreams about. I envy him that his morning has been so peaceful while mine is shaping up as a minor nightmare. As it usually does these days, the trouble began with my thirteen-year-old son, Jonathan.

It started when I caught him dropping gobs of gooey hair gel on my antique mahogany table while using the mirror above it.

"If I've told you once, I've told you a thousand times . . ." I exploded. Once again we were bickering—me nagging and controlling, my son resentful and defiant. Hearing the whine of the school bus outside, I rudely pushed him out the door. I noticed Jonathan's thin shoulders sagging a little as he ran. *Good,* I thought, *maybe I've gotten through to him this time.*

Then later this morning came another call from the dean of students at my son's junior high school.

"Mrs. Smyth," he began hesitantly, "I know you've probably come to dread these reports as much as I do, but we've had another incident here you must be told about."

What now? I wondered helplessly. My mind raced over the catalog of recent transgressions Jonathan had committed. *He wasn't always like this.*

"In science class this morning," the dean said, clearing his throat, "Jonathan was carrying on and sprayed another boy's shirt with iodine. He must stay for detention and, of course, that shirt will have to be paid for."

My face burned with embarrassment and rage as I hung up the phone. The money Jonathan had been saving for new hockey gear would now go for the boy's shirt. That much I knew. But I was at a loss to understand what was happening to Jonathan, or what to do about it. Jonathan's adolescence had hit us like a tidal surge. When I wasn't quarreling with Jonathan, I was worrying about him, resenting this newfound obnoxiousness.

I try to shake off the morning's traumas and turn my attention back to the slumbering Roscoe. He has a public appearance to make. Roscoe is a Guiding Eyes puppy, and I have agreed to raise him until he's ready for formal guide dog training. I was warned by his breeders that he was the dominant pup of his litter and will be a real handful once he begins to assert himself. So far he has been a dream.

An hour later I am seated on a folding chair in front of an elementary school gymnasium filled with giggling, squirming children. They crane their heads for a peek at the sleek puppy on my lap. Roscoe's dark eyes casually scan his little fans. I glance at the grown-up guide dog sitting tall beside her blind owner next to me. "That is what you will be like when you grow up," I whisper into Roscoe's soft puppy ear. He steals a kiss and wags his tail.

We begin the program with Kathy from Guiding Eyes explaining my role as a puppy raiser. She tells the children that I will steer my dog from puppy-hood through adolescence. I am to love and discipline him, teach him manners and basic commands and, when he is older, take him to public places such as restaurants and office buildings.

While Kathy talks, Roscoe chews his teething ring placidly. The children laugh at him because he has suddenly fallen asleep and is snoring loudly. Roscoe awakes with a start, bewildered, and cocks an ear.

I look out at their fresh-scrubbed faces. They seem so eager and coopera-tive, like Jonathan before he turned thirteen. There he is in my mind again. Jonathan. I am always brooding about what he used to be like or what I wish he would be like now. It's not so much what he does, but the belligerence he does it with. Yes, sometimes he is the same sweet kid I've always known. Usually he is. But other times he is moody, defiant. I hate the person I am becoming. I always seem to be carrying a grudge against my son, like today. I am anxious for him to come home from school so we can have it out about that boy's shirt.

Roscoe shifts in my lap and I snap back to the program. Audrey, the blind lady, is demonstrating how her dog, Eva, makes it possible for her to live virtually a normal life. The children are hushed with amazement. "Forward!" Audrey commands. Eva confidently leads her through a maze of chairs and around a grand piano. "Good girl!" There is a burst of applause. Roscoe sits up groggily and wags his tail. He believes the clapping is for him.

"No, Roscoe," I say softly. "Someday people will applaud you, but we have a long road ahead of us."

On the way home Roscoe whimpers in his crate. He is demanding to sit on my lap while I drive. This is not the Roscoe who came from the breeder a few days ago.

"No," I say firmly, keeping my eyes on the street.

The whimpering quickly escalates to a high-pitched yowl. I slap the top of the crate with a loud whop. This behavior must be discouraged. Roscoe stops—temporarily. We battle all the way home and I begin to understand the breeder's warning. Roscoe is a strong-willed pup!

After lunch I can't find Roscoe. I call his name and whistle. Suddenly I hear a terrible racket in the next room and race toward it. Roscoe has cornered Sheba, our cat, who deftly springs to a table. "Roscoe, no!" I yell, joining the chase. Ignoring my command, Roscoe bounds after her, bouncing up and down from the floor. *Crash.* My beautiful African violets in their prized hand-painted vase splatter in a broken mess. Roscoe, the unrepentant, dives gleefully through the dirt, smearing it into the rug. I am appalled by his behavior: "Bad dog!" I shout.

His eyes gleam up at me triumphantly, challengingly. I think back to what the puppy manual advises about dominance. Be firm, it says, be patient. And always follow punishment with praise. Roscoe complies with my order to sit. Then I praise him to the skies. He is his old puppy self again.

I scoop him up and return him to his crate. Immediately he begins to whine; soon it is a full-blown tantrum. I need some peace, so I head off to the library. I won't be gone long. I want to be back when Jonathan gets home. I haven't forgotten what happened in science class.

When I return I hear Roscoe still carrying on upstairs. My temper is about to explode. It blows sky high when I reach the crate. Roscoe has completely torn apart his little domain. I yank him out of the crate, put him down on the floor and yell something I don't mean: "You will never ever make it as a guide dog! I don't want you anymore!"

This time Roscoe hangs his head in shame. His ears draw back and his tail droops. He is truly sorry. But I am still angry with his willfulness. He must learn to control himself. "You can't keep testing me like this," I complain. As I stomp away Roscoe follows meekly at my heels. He won't let me out of his sight. It strikes me that the little puppy needs me more now than ever. He seems to understand this somehow.

Suddenly a phrase from another manual comes to mind, the "manual" of love:

Love never gives up.

It is from 1 Corinthians 13 (TEV), and it is just another way of saying that love always gives second chances. How many have I had from God? Too many to count!

Love does not keep a record of wrongs. Another line from 1 Corinthians. I stop and look out the window. In the distance I see the late school bus making its way up the street. I've been wrangling with Roscoe all day long, but deep in my heart I have also been wrangling with Jonathan, fighting the resentment that was left hanging in the air after our argument this morning, resentment I have not let go of. I *have* been keeping a record, a bitter record, of all of my son's wrongs.

Jonathan, I think, is trying to find his feet in life. It is a process we all go through, and it is not always pleasant. Strangely, in his search for independence, Jonathan needs me more than ever. He needs me to be firm yet patient, to help him find his way through a terribly difficult period. It is a learning process for us both, but he will never again be the little boy he was. He is growing up, and more than ever my love must give second chances.

I feel Roscoe leaning comfortably against my ankle. I look down and give him a rub on his head. "I'm sorry," I say. Something in his eyes reveals that he understands me, and he will try to do better.

A few minutes later the front door opens and closes. Jonathan stands in the doorway to the kitchen, tossing his gel-styled hair defiantly. He is braced for a lecture loaded with wrongs from his recent past. I surprise him, and myself. "Why did you do it?" I ask simply.

He studies me silently then sits down at the table and stares out the window. I strain to hear his answer.

"I don't know," he says, "I just wasn't thinking."

It is an honest answer, not an excuse. He shifts uncomfortably and volunteers that the right thing to do is pay for the shirt with his own money and write an apology.

Before he leaves I feel compelled to say something good about him. When I think about it, it is not hard. There are many, many good things about Jonathan. "Your dad and I appreciate how considerate you are about letting us know where you're going and when you're coming home."

Jon looks away in embarrassment and gets up to go to his room and study. As he leaves, I am full of love and pride for my son.

It is nighttime. Roscoe is asleep again, snoring in his little crate. Jon comes into the kitchen. He piddles around, then looks at me steadily. "Mom," he says, "I really am sorry."

"Me too," I gulp.

Quickly, before I can hug him, he's off to bed.

Dear Lord, I pray, *thank You for showing us how to wipe the slate clean.*

AIMING AT PERFECTION
Phyllis Hobe

"No!" the trainer said. I stopped immediately and Kate sat crookedly at my side, biting playfully at the leash that dangled from my hand.

Mr. Magill scowled at us. Slowly he walked around us, pointed at my feet and Kate's paws. "They should be in a line," he said. "She's off to one side and three inches in front of you."

I thought he was a bit picky, and I guess he read my mind. "What we're after is perfection," he said. "Nothing less."

I flinched. Somehow I never thought of trying to train my dog perfectly!

"There's a reason," Mr. Magill explained. "It only takes one car to hit your dog. It only takes one moment, when you don't have control of Kate, for her to lose her life. Perfection in these exercises isn't for appearances—it's for your dog's safety. You've got to demand more of her—and of yourself."

That was all he said. That was all I needed to make me take our training more seriously. I took a step forward, said "Heel!" in a commanding voice, and Kate came lumbering to my side. "She's slouching," Mr. Magill commented. Obviously we had work to do.

I used to think God was asking too much of us when He said we should be perfect. But I'm beginning to understand what He meant. Perfection isn't for show. It's for our own well-being; it protects us from some of the sins in life. And it takes a lot of hard work.

COMMUNICATING WITH KATE
Phyllis Hobe

Today once again I was practicing the command for Kate to come to me from a distance. There she sat at the end of a long leash, just as proper as could be—and the moment I would call, "Kate, come!" she'd veer off in another direction after a squirrel, a falling leaf or a friendly neighbor. I was ready to quit.

But then I found myself smiling. Wasn't Kate just like me, going off in all different directions while God is right in front of me, waiting for me to come to Him? But He never gives up on me.

"Okay, Kate," I said, scratching her under the chin, "We're going to keep at this until we get it right."

It took a few more days, but one day when I called, Kate bounded straight to me. "Heel!" I said, and she whipped around my side, looking up at me eagerly. She seemed to realize what we were trying to accomplish. I was so happy. Our hard work was making it possible for us to communicate with each other!

Now I think I know a little bit about how God feels when I finally do something right.

OUT OF SHAPE

Walter Harter

My dachshund Phoebe is seven years old. She's my constant companion, a lovable creature. I hadn't realized how fat and lazy she had become until one day she couldn't get out of her basket. The vet gave me a stern lecture. "This dog is obese. No doubt," he surmised correctly, "you feed her what you eat. She needs exercise. Get her a companion, a puppy to play with."

So Phoebe became a substitute mother to our newest addition, Hans, a small red dachshund. (His complete name is Hans Ludwig van Beethoven!) As she plays and runs with the puppy, I can almost see the pounds falling from her body.

One day I stopped to look at myself. "I'm as out of shape as Phoebe. Little exercise, little interest in anything. I certainly need help." When I confided in my wife, Edna, she suggested that God might want me to help someone else in the process: "How about being a Big Brother?" This organization, which matches up adults with boys who need substitute fathers, is active in my area.

I'm now a Big Brother. I see my young friend for a couple of hours every weekend, and we make quite a foursome—Phoebe, Hans, Tom and I. I eat healthy food (so does Phoebe), and if the exercise we get playing games with Tom hasn't made my excess pounds melt away, I do feel better. Best of all, I love the feeling of affection that Tom and I have for each other.

OBEDIENCE AND SERENITY

James McDermott

The phone call on Saturday from the Port Washington, Long Island, train stationmaster came as a surprise. "There's a dog here in a crate," he told my father, "addressed to you." And, sure enough, when we got to the station, there was a beautiful Llewellyn setter, shivering with fear, inside a big wooden crate. It later turned out that my grandfather had trained the dog and sent her to us from Virginia, but had forgotten to notify us.

My father borrowed a crowbar from the stationmaster and began to pry the crate open. He had taken three boards off when the dog bolted out and tore down the railroad tracks. My father frantically looked for a shipping tag with the dog's name on it and, finding it, muttered, "Ah, it's Victoria." Hearing her name, even in that whisper, our new dog stopped dead in her tracks and came back to us, tentatively wagging her tail.

In her eleven years with us, "Vickie" was an adored member of our family. Although we never made the slightest attempt to refresh her on the training she had received, she never lost a bit of her original obedience. In fact, she seemed to thrive on it. She was the happiest, most serene dog I have ever encountered.

Since then I've often thought that her obedience was the key to her serenity. And I believe our Creator had our contentment in mind when He handed down our most important Commandments. The more closely I adhere to them, the happier I am.

II

Little Pet Lost

Trustful Waiting

Scott Harrison

Sam was my best dog, ever. A field trial dog who found birds and pointed them with contagious enthusiasm, Sam taught me the joy of becoming part of nature. If his point said a bird was hiding in a clump of bushes, it was there. He was much more than a bird dog, though. Often we'd share together lazy lunches in an abandoned apple orchard, and the snooze that followed.

Late one afternoon, Sam and I became separated. Neither of us was familiar with the area. I called and whistled. No sign of Sam. I had to get back to town for an important appointment. But how could I leave Sam? If he finally came back and I wasn't there, would I lose him for good?

Then I remembered a trick an old dog trainer had passed on. I unbuttoned my jacket, removed my shirt and laid it on the ground under the branches of a small bush.

I worried all night. But when I returned the next morning, there was Sam curled up with his nose under the sleeve of my shirt. He looked up and wagged his tail. "Where've you been, friend?" his eyes seemed to say. "I've been waiting for you all night. But I knew you'd come back."

Later I wondered. When I get lost, do I have the trust to look for some part of God's word and curl up in it? To wait patiently, knowing that my Friend will find me if I just have faith in Him?

Rescue

Marion Bond West

Although I agreed to go shopping with one of my closest friends, I didn't really want to go. My husband had died only a week earlier and I was grieving.

As we drove down the highway, Jo Ann and I both saw the dog at the same time. It was weaving in and out of the traffic, and horns were blaring from all directions at the poor confused animal. But it ignored the cars almost as though it would welcome not having to struggle any longer. The temperature was a hundred degrees, and the dog appeared about ready to have a heat stroke. Gaunt, lost, and hopeless, it staggered along on a hot pavement, limping.

"Please stop, Jo Ann!" I cried suddenly.

I named the dog Hannah even before we got back to my house with her. For a long time she stared at me as if in disbelief, before lowering her head to devour the food I set before her. I filled the water dish twice. Caleb, our collie, gave Hannah a friendly lick. Later, at the veterinarian's office she received the best of care. The cut in her foot healed nicely. And her fear of people, and of pain left her. She began to wag her tail. Then one day she jumped up and nestled in my lap in absolute delight and trust. There were times when I actually thought I saw Hannah smile!

Finally it seemed as though her desperate fear had fully melted into desperate gratitude. I know now that I brought Hannah home because I identified with her obvious need for comfort and healing. At one time life hadn't seemed worth the effort for either of us.

We were wrong—Hannah and I.

Praying for Pete's Sake

Bonnie Swartz

R-r-r-ruufff, rr-r-ruff-ruff. Even the family pets seemed to be stirred up by the big blizzard just arriving in our southeast corner of Michigan! I turned from the kitchen window to see Boots, our spunky rat terrier, streaking after Pete the parakeet, who was zooming toward his open cage like a tiny green-and-yellow guided missile.

"I'm going to put you two in the circus," I told them. Whenever we left the door of Pete's cage open to give him an outing, he liked to swoop down and perch between Boots' ears—one black, one white—and give him a few friendly pecks. With the bird on the dog's head, they looked like the top of a totem pole.

Usually Boots put up with Pete's antics, but today he kept chasing Pete back to his birdcage. Then a few minutes later Pete would sneak out and peck Boots again.

If I hadn't been so busy getting our household ready for the bad weather I'd have enjoyed watching the pair of them. Forecasts of heavy snow and high winds had been coming over the radio since the night before. "Better stock up on milk and candles," my husband, Ron, had warned. So all morning I'd checked supplies and shopped and cooked.

I looked out the window again, keeping an eye on my little girls—three blue-eyed blondes and three dark-eyed brunettes—their ages stair-stepped from twelve to six. The local schools had closed at noon because of the blizzard alert, and now all six children were playing in the backyard. Enough snow had fallen already to cover the ground and I could tell the wind off nearby Lake Erie was picking up. As I watched them, the girls began a snowball fight, and the first thing you know Judith, the youngest, almost got hit in the face. She ran toward the house to complain to me and just as she yanked open the door it happened. Boots started to chase Pet and *swish!* Pete flew out the door.

It was so quick that I stood still for a moment in shock. That tiny handful of feathers couldn't stand bitter cold weather for long! I grabbed a coat and ran out to try to get Pete back into the house before he froze to death.

Swirls of snow eddied around my feet as I dashed across the yard, trying to follow the little green-and-yellow blur. Pete flew to the big black walnut tree and lighted on a branch.

I stood beneath, calling to him in a wheedling voice. The girls gathered around me and added their pleas.

Pete's answer was to fly off again, this time heading down Arbor Avenue. We all took off after him, seven of us stringing out behind him like the tail of a kite. When he landed again, it was in a tree almost a block away.

"Here, Petie. Come down, sweet Pete; come down here. Oh, please come down?"

He looked so huddled and frightened, but he paid no attention to us. Finally, he fluttered his wings again and this time we couldn't follow him any farther in the snow. He flew out of sight. As we stood there looking helplessly into the empty, snow-dimmed sky, the wind began to blow harder. The blizzard was here in force.

That evening after dinner we sat around the table as usual while the girls took turns saying their prayers. Theresa, Kathleen, Anne, Susan, Patricia, Judith—one after the other, they said pretty much the same thing, "Please God, take care of Petie out in the storm." I looked at Ron glumly. I knew Pete could not survive the weather he had gone into. But I said nothing to my children.

The next morning snow was piled so high in our driveway and on Arbor Avenue that we couldn't leave the house all day. Even so, the girls continued to expect Pete to come home. Once more, they said their prayers, confident that their pet was safe. After they were asleep that night, I asked Ron what we should do. "We always taught them to pray and have faith, but this is going to be an awful letdown. I *know* Pete died in the storm."

"Do you think we should buy another parakeet and try to pass it off as Pete?" he mused.

I thought for a minute. "No, we shouldn't try to fool them. Besides, Pete was too special—they'd know any other parakeet wasn't him." I sighed. "I guess we should just pray that they'll accept the fact that he's gone—and not be too heartbroken."

The third day after the blizzard, things began to get back to normal. Most of the roads were plowed and people were out clearing their sidewalks and exchanging stories about their experiences during the storm. My daughters told everyone about their pet being out in the blizzard. "But he'll fly back soon," they'd say. Even Boots managed to look hopeful as he sat under the empty birdcage, his head cocked expectantly.

The waiting ended late that afternoon. Kathleen, my eleven-year-old, darted up to me in the kitchen waving *The Monroe Evening News*, her eyes as round as pennies. She was so excited she couldn't talk, just spread out the Classified Page and pointed. "Found, Yellow and Green Parakeet."

After we called the number given in the ad, we put together the highlights of Pete's incredible adventure:

• In the teeth of the blizzard, he had flown (or been blown) a mile and a half across the icebound Raisin River.

• This flight terminated at a familiar landing field—the neck of a dog chained in the yard behind a house.

• His foot became entangled in the dog's collar, causing the dog to begin barking and jumping.

• Alerted by the commotion, the dog's owner came outside to investigate and discovered Pete.

She calmly freed the bird and took him inside. Finding that one of his legs was frozen stiff, she was wise enough to hold Pete in the palm of her hand till it thawed.

You see, this woman to whom Pete was safely delivered was not merely a kind soul but a person who had dedicated her life to caring for animals—an employee of the local Humane Society.

Our girls were not in the least surprised when they heard how elaborately their prayers had been answered. "*See*, Mom?" they choroused.

See? I knew how Saul felt when the scales fell from his eyes.

My daughters had prayed for Pete's life. I assumed he was dead. My daughters trusted that God would take care of Pete. I didn't even *hope* for the bird's survival, let alone believe in it . . .

Sometimes a well-meaning mother's "practical knowledge" gets in the way of her faith. When that happened to me, God used six little girls, five feet of snow and a feisty tropical bird to remind me of the power of prayer.

I think He did it with a smile, don't you?

Lost and Found

Of course, the world's not coming to an end
Because one sassy little parakeet
Flew out the door last night. No use to spend
Tears on a bit of feathery conceit
Who'll make a tasty morsel for a cat
And won't be pulling anybody's hair
Or nibbling books they read, again. What's that?
Somebody's found a bird? Where is he? Where?
My word, he's got tar on him! Frowsy-feathered,
And nearly starved, almost too weak to fly,
He's wholly unsubdued by all he's weathered,
With the old puckish glint still in his eye.
Bring him on in, and double latch that door;
The world can wag upon its way once more.

—— *Jane Merchant*

Jasper, Yoda and Jesus

Margie Nadine Walker

I silently prayed for wisdom as I watched my twelve-year-old daughter, Kris, print these words on a large cardboard sign: Lost—Black Kitten—Named "Yoda"—$10 Reward. For the past four days after school, we had canvassed the neighborhood door to door, posted signs and placed a "lost kitten" ad in the paper. Then, hoping to catch a glimpse of him, we walked and drove up and down the surrounding streets. But Yoda had disappeared.

From the very beginning, as soon as we discovered he was gone, we had prayed for Yoda. Now, as our little girl began to realize that we probably would never see him again, I yearned to find reassuring words to tell her. "Please, God," I prayed, "don't let her faith in You be shattered because of this. What can I say to her if we can't find her kitten?"

Our family's adventure with cats had started two years earlier, when *we*—yes, *we*—were adopted by a large, older, striped-gray cat, whom we named Jasper. He was "king" of the backyard, very dignified, and for the past two years had reigned supreme over the neighborhood. Appearing to be hostile and gruff, he was really putty in our hands, gentle and loving.

One day I jokingly pointed out to my husband that what Jasper needed was a little kitten to play with (preferably black, because Kris and I loved black cats—they're so sleek and shiny . . . and special!). And guess what? I had just found one in a "free kitten" ad. Larry, who was not a cat lover, shook his head. "Jasper'll never accept another cat," he said. "I think you're just asking for trouble." But he didn't object, so Kris and I answered the ad and went to pick him up.

The kitten was hiding in a corner of the garage in a laundry basket. He was solid black, with a tiny nick on his chin. Kris loved him instantly. We took him home and named him "Yoda," for an outer-space character in the *Star Wars* movie series.

In the first several days, Yoda settled into our family with no effort at all. He was an adventurous kitten who liked to ride in our car with us and loved to ride in the basket of Kris's bicycle.

But Jasper did not take easily to the newcomer. He seemed insulted to have his domain threatened and was prone to ignore Yoda, only looking up to hiss as Yoda slid into feeding time like a baseball player stealing second. Undaunted, Yoda treated Jasper like his dearly loved older brother, always running expectantly toward him and trying to play with him. Yoda's day was complete when he could snuggle up beside Jasper on the crocheted afghan,

Yoda, god created man and all the world. See the farm land up ahead god created exry grain of wheat over there.

kneading it with his paws and purring himself to sleep. Never mind that Jasper, ever superior, totally ignored him.

It was about this time that Kris, who was always quick to express herself through art, started drawing cartoons about the two cats. Kris believed that when we weren't watching them, Jasper played with Yoda, giving him advice, taking pleasure in his company. And so Kris's drawings showed a kindly older cat telling the "new cat on the block" important things about life on Earth, things like God's love and the need to pray and sing praises. There were cartoons of Jasper wearing a cape and flying through the sky on secret missions, with Yoda on his back, showing him the wonders of God's creation. From that time on we dubbed him "Bat Cat."

In the second week or so, I began to think that maybe Kris had the right idea: I'd see Jasper watching Yoda intently, his ears pitched forward. Occasionally I even saw him batting Yoda playfully with his paws, and once I caught him bathing Yoda's face—but *never* when Jasper thought I was watching.

Now Yoda you don't tell anyone that I said this to you, but did you know god loves you and he made you just as he wanted? Well he does and you should pray with him each night and sing praise unto his name! Now flow run along before somone catches me talking to you !!!

This was the state of affairs when, about six weeks later, Yoda, not wearing his identifying collar, wandered away, probably chasing a butterfly. Kris and I were heartbroken.

And so the search began. With each fruitless day that passed, we continued to hope and make plans for the next day. "Tomorrow we'll try this . . . or that," we said. But soon we had looked everywhere with no sign of the lost kitten. I put my arm around Kris as she buried her face in my shoulder, not wanting me to see her tears. "Mom, if I could just know that someone was taking care of him," she said. "Or if he had to die, at least know he didn't suffer. I could even accept it if he found a good home, with someone who loved cats the way we do. But I just keep picturing him out there . . . all alone . . . and it hurts so bad."

"This cat has got to go back to earth...he's causing a great disturbance!"

I knew exactly how she felt and realized then that I was worried not only about Yoda but about Kris as well. *I need help, Lord,* I prayed silently. *Just give me wisdom. I can't carry this alone anymore, so I'm giving it all to You. Please help me trust You and find words now that will help Kris.*

Turning to her, I began, "Kris, we *must* give this problem to Jesus. He cares, and He really is the only One who knows the total situation. Can you believe—*even* if you never see Yoda again—that he just went for a walk with Jesus? Can you trust that Jesus will take care of him?"

We prayed together then. Just a simple prayer, asking Jesus to take care of Yoda. And I hugged Kris.

I really didn't expect what happened next. Kris's face lit up for the first time in days and she raced from the room. Cartoons began flying off her notebook paper again, as she grasped the concept of a little black cat "going for a walk with Jesus."

There were pictures of Jesus and Yoda—riding a bike together, frolicking through heaven (to the dismay of several angels), exhaustedly taking a nap on the clouds and then sitting at the table eating together.

So clearly did these drawings reflect her happiness—and faith—that as she shared them with me, we began to laugh, and then cry at the same time. It was with complete trust that Kris said, "Mom, it's okay. I know that if I never see Yoda again, Jesus will take care of him."

Yes, I thought, *it is okay.* Only God could have chosen such a unique way of answering my prayer. What a beautiful reminder that, no matter what my own problems, God will always have a custom-designed, just-for-me answer.

Then, ten days after Yoda disappeared, a telephone call came from Mary Simms, a "cat-loving" woman who had just read our ad in the weekly paper. We rushed over to find Yoda happily playing on the patio with her cats—on what looked like a feline gymnasium.

Together we learned that, to get to her house, Yoda had crossed three very busy main streets, had traveled one and a half miles (in a direction we hadn't even looked) and had narrowly missed being hit by several cars, as his rescuer watched helplessly from her kitchen window.

Many times Mary had attempted to coax him from his hiding place with food, but having been chased into thick ivy by dogs, Yoda was terrified. Finally she was able to rescue the starving kitten and take him home with her.

A peek into our home that evening, after we brought Yoda back, would have revealed quite a scene. As Yoda was put down on the floor, a look of wonderment crossed his face. He looked around and sniffed the air for a few minutes. Suddenly he ran toward the kitchen and slid into the feeding dish like a baseball player stealing second. Yes, Jasper was there, but this time he licked Yoda's face as if to say, "Welcome home."

Later we put the two cats in the garage, where they always slept at night in baskets on top of the chest freezer. Next morning, on his way to the car, Larry let the cats into the house. As Kris and I bent to kiss them, we were met with the lingering odor of . . . after-shave lotion! . . . wafting from their foreheads. We just looked at each other and smiled.

12

Growing Old Together

No Complaining

Van Varner

Both my dog Clay and I are getting old and arthritic. In dog years, Clay's a lot older than I and maybe he's more arthritic too (at least I can still climb up on the bed without being boosted). No, my arthritis is the mild kind that moves around from my left hip to my fingers to the heel of my right foot with just enough pain to make me complain about it. And that's exactly what I was doing—complaining—to a friend of mine recently when she said, "Why can't you be more like your dog?"

I couldn't tell whether she was being serious or sarcastic—or both. "Meaning what?" I asked.

"Well, does Clay complain about *his* arthritis?"

I've been watching Clay lately and there's something to my friend's comment. On our long walks in the morning, Clay will trot ahead of me, his ears at half-alert, the soles of his paws flicking back like the hoofs of a race horse, his tail swinging pleasurably from side to side, when suddenly, without any warning, those old legs of his will give way and he'll go crashing down into the dirt, a startled look of noncomprehension in his eyes. I'll rush to help him but before I can get there, he'll be up again and back on the trail, the tail swinging pleasurably as though nothing had happened. No complaining. No feeling sorry for himself.

Come on, Van, take a tip from your old dog Clay. Stop complaining, get up, get on with the joyous business of living!

SEEING-EYE PERSON

Arthur Gordon

A letter came today from our friend George who lives in the shadow of the Whitestone Bridge on the edge of New York City. In one paragraph he talks about his friend Co-co.

Co-co is a big chocolate-colored poodle, the most remarkable dog I've ever met. Whenever we'd come to visit, Co-co would astonish us by seeming to understand every word George said to her. If he wanted his shoes from upstairs, she'd go and get them. If they were the wrong pair, she'd take them back and bring the right one. If George said, "Robber!" or "Crook!" she'd go tearing around the house to make sure there were no intruders. Now and then I'd see Co-co and George looking at each other with affectionate amusement, as if they shared a joke that none of the rest of us could understand.

But the years go by, and now George's letter says—and I know it was painful for him to write—that Co-co has gone blind. "We've evolved a way of looping her leash (which she hasn't worn in years) loosely around her shoulders, and with this she walks confidently by my side. I can steer her either way with the slightest pressure. So here I am, a seeing-eye person for a blind dog."

Now on afternoons like today with so many angry headlines in the paper and so many small problems crowding in, I somehow find it both touching and heartening to think of my friend George and his friend Co-co walking along tranquilly and trustfully, side by side. And I know the leash is only a symbol of the real bond between them.

The real bond is love.

LOOKING OUT FOR TROOPER

Phyllis Hobe

My dog Trooper is thirteen years old. Among animals, he's a real senior citizen.

Trooper can't do a lot of the things that he used to do. He's almost totally deaf now and he doesn't hear people when they come to the door. It embarrasses him when they suddenly appear and he barks—even at friends whom he knows. It's his way of insisting that he's still looking out for me, and I appreciate that.

But now that Trooper is old, I find that I look out for him too. I don't like to leave him at home alone for more than a few hours at a time. And when I'm away, if he's outdoors and it begins to rain, I dash home to give him shelter. For years he has followed me from room to room. Now when I'm going to another part of the house, I tap him on the shoulder to let him know that I'm on the move. He wants to be with me and I enjoy his company. We're old friends and time isn't going to change that.

Some people say that having a pet is too much trouble. "You get so attached to them," they tell me.

Maybe so. But maybe love means that you allow yourself to get attached. I would like to think that when I'm on in years, the people I love will feel attached to me.

You Don't Say Goodbye

Phyllis Hobe

How do you say good-bye to such a good friend?

Trooper has been with me for fourteen years, since he was a puppy with glazed newborn eyes. Now his eyes are glazed again, but with oncoming blindness. Not only is he deaf, but his hind legs are stiff with arthritis.

Two years ago I almost lost him to a liver ailment. The rest of my world was falling apart then, too, and I knew I couldn't handle such a loss. But Trooper recovered, much to the astonishment of the veterinarians. And sadly I knew that one day I would have to let Trooper have his rest.

Now the day has come when it is time to let him go. His sense of smell is gone. He can no longer identify those he knows, and every approaching footstep is a threat to him. I can't allow my dignified, loving friend to be destroyed by fear and confusion. . . .

The doctor was compassionate. I stayed with Trooper until the end, which was gentle.

How do you say good-bye to such a friend? You don't. You weep, and you let God share your tears. And you thank Him for the love that came into your life—because you know now that that part of your friend will be with you forever.

My Friend Mollie

Marion Bond West

*T*he instant my husband walked toward me I knew something was terribly wrong. I'd been away all day at a seminar. It was now late afternoon.

"Mollie's hurt bad," Jerry said simply and quickly. I think I let out a low moan. Then I began asking questions. Early in the morning, just after I left, our beloved four-year-old collie had been hit by a car and seriously hurt.

In my mind I saw it happening. I didn't want to watch, but I couldn't stop the vivid pictures. Jerry had stayed home from work on a Friday to catch up on yard work and to be with our thirteen-year-old twin sons while I was at the meeting. Thoughts of *if only I hadn't gone* began. I tried to force them away.

Mollie hurt. I couldn't yet believe it. Memories of the first time I saw her eased into my racing mind. It was sweet relief from the horrible pictures of her darting out in front of the car.

After our seventeen-year-old mutt Muff had to be put to sleep with disorders of old age, we didn't talk about dogs much, even though we are dog people. Then one fall I mentioned to Jerry in a casual way that I'd been thinking about getting another dog. A collie. I suggested it almost hesitantly, knowing what loving another dog would involve. I almost hoped he'd say no. He beamed, "I've been thinking the same thing. A collie for Christmas." We searched the want ads that day and then drove out to see some collie pups. There were four left. Jerry picked up the best looking one. While he held it, a smaller and more timid puppy came up to him and laid her head on his foot. She didn't make a sound. He put down the frisky pup and picked up the shy one. She laid her head on his shoulder, glancing once at him briefly. "The other dog is finer," my husband announced weakly.

"I know," I stroked the long-nosed puppy, "but he's not for us, is he? This one is." When we learned the puppy's mother had Love as her middle name, we named our choice "For the Love of Mollie." The people we bought her from kept her until Christmas Eve so she could be a surprise for Jon and Jeremy and our teenage girls, Julie and Jennifer.

When I saw Mollie again it was Christmas Eve and Jerry was bringing her into the kitchen with a big bow around her neck. She seemed afraid and unsure of our love and acceptance, but uncomplaining—hopeful. I was afraid and unsure too that night. Our seventeen-year-old daughter Julie had just become engaged. I knew I had to give her up. Perhaps that's why I clung to

Mollie with such deep needs. From the beginning I loved the dog far too much. Eventually our entire family did.

She grew into a majestic beauty, but even more beautiful was her spirit. Content in our large backyard, her world, she never wanted to venture out without permission. She fancied herself a guardian to those she loved. Often she tried to impress us and make us believe she'd chased off some terrible enemy. She barked at airplanes and turned around joyfully for our approval when she saw that she had "driven" the planes away. We always praised her. After a bath, she would run like a race dog around and around the yard, then tumble into one of us. During the hot Georgia summers, one of the boys filled up our yellow wheelbarrow with water, and Mollie immediately hopped in and dunked her head. She could hold her breath for a long time and would look up at us from beneath the water with a comical expression on her face.

Gentle beyond all comprehension, she romped with our cats and chased them, only to let them escape. One of her favorite sleeping spots was the back steps. When I opened the door to allow the cats to come in or out, they simply walked over Mollie as though she were a huge sable-and-white door mat. She would raise her head and look with approval. If one of the cats wanted in on cold nights, Mollie learned to throw herself against the door and open it, allowing the cat to enter. But she would not come in herself until someone said, "Okay." Then she would bound in and down into the den as though it had been months since she'd seen us. Before she went back out she usually ate the cats' food while the cats watched, seeming almost to approve.

We often took her on family walks through the woods. How she loved it, charging ahead of us, then circling back to check on us. I suppose my favorite times with her were early in the morning. I would go outside before seven and sit on the back step in my nightgown. She would come up and lay her head in my lap the way she did the first time she saw Jerry. The world smelled wonderful and new and moist. I would tell her, "I love you, Mollie Sunshine." She would look right into my eyes and wag her magnificent tail. I know she understood. And her love was always totally unconditional and never changing.

She had no fear of cars. She assumed that everything that moved loved her as we did. Her only fears seemed to be thunder and the garbage man. She barked at him each week, looking over her shoulder at me as if telling me that she would protect us.

It had happened so suddenly. Jerry had been cutting the front grass and had let her out to walk alongside him. He took his eyes off her for an instant, and she darted into the street. She'd done it before, but there was so little traffic on our street. This time, she picked the wrong minute to investigate something on the other side of the road. We were critical of people who let their animals roam. We rescued stray dogs from the highway. How could this have happened to our Mollie, right in front of our house?

My husband said she didn't cry out or struggle as he ran to her. She appeared relaxed, almost apologetic as he took her to the vet, five minutes away. X-rays revealed a badly fractured hip and pelvis and a broken tail. Her tail would have to be removed during surgery. It was broken where it joined her body.

"Well, why aren't they operating now?" I questioned.

"We have to wait until Monday to see if her bowels and bladder are working. The vet said he has to know that before surgery can be done. He has an orthopedic vet ready to do the surgery Monday morning."

"When can I see her?"

"Tomorrow. They're closed now."

Thoughts of Mollie alone at the clinic tormented me. I phoned around until I located the vet and asked him countless questions. I didn't really listen to his answers. I wanted him to assure me she would be fine. He didn't. He told me that I could see her early in the morning. I didn't sleep well. I prayed that Mollie was sleeping comfortably in her cage. When I slept, I dreamed she was running through our backyard again—without her tail—but nevertheless running, barking at planes, guarding us.

The next morning we waited for the clinic to open. Suddenly the vet was bringing Mollie to us. She looked alert. The vet brought her outside to see if she'd go to the bathroom in the grass. Jerry and I fell to our knees and put our arms around her. We talked to her and asked her questions. I suppose vets get used to people like us. She sat erect, looking almost normal. She watched a plane overhead, but did not bark. "I love you, Mollie Sunshine," I whispered.

The vet assured us, "She's not in pain. I've never seen a dog so broken up in so little discomfort."

"Well, we have been praying and asking God not to let her hurt."

The vet nodded. "That's it then. Try to keep her moving," he said over his shoulder as he went back inside to the busy clinic. For over two hours we hoped Mollie would go to the bathroom. Nothing happened. Finally the vet suggested we take her home for the weekend. Perhaps, at home, she would relieve herself in her own backyard.

At home Jerry took her to her beloved backyard—her world. He laid her in a favorite spot—under a large oak tree. The cats, Joshua and Jessica, came over to rub against her. She gobbled up everything I gave her to eat. I didn't bother with dog food. She got steak, hamburger, roast beef. As it became hotter and the gnats and flies bothered her, we brought her into the cool den by the fireplace, another of her favorite spots. She looked perfectly normal lying there, as though she might bound up the steps any minute.

Surely by tomorrow she would relieve herself and we could go ahead with plans for the surgery. It was going to be an expensive operation. We decided to cancel our upcoming vacation in order to have the money for the surgery and then to be at home with Mollie and take care of her.

By Saturday night she still hadn't gone to the bathroom. She would lick her paws and groom herself after eating. She couldn't reach her hind part, so it began to look a bit rumpled. I would brush it, and she would appear in good shape again. Our married daughter Julie came by to see her. Julie had worked for the vet who was treating Mollie. Mollie lifted her head high as she recognized Julie bending over her. Since she couldn't wag her tail, she sort of gave Julie a smile. Julie knelt for a long time and didn't say anything. "Looks good, doesn't she?" I asked hopefully.

Still looking at Mollie, Julie answered softly, "No, Mama. She's putting on a brave, wonderful front for you. See how tired her eyes are. It will be highly unusual if she comes through this. I've seen this type of injury before." Julie got up and walked upstairs without looking back. After Julie and her husband left, I went back into the den. Mollie put her head in my lap. She sighed and looked deep into my eyes. She wasn't smiling. My tears came suddenly and unexpectedly, and deep agony exploded inside me like a volcano. My tears spilled onto Mollie's face so that she blinked her eyes. Jerry came and sat by me. We didn't say anything. We just held Mollie and made terrible noises crying.

Sunday morning we got up and went immediately to the den. Mollie was unmoved, like a statue. I decided that I simply could not leave her and go to church that morning. The rest of the family stayed home too.

On Monday morning Jerry gathered Mollie in his arms and put her back under the oak tree. She looked perfectly content. A plane flew overhead, and she looked up. One of the cats came over and lay by her in the grass. I began to pray that Mollie would give up. I couldn't watch her try so hard anymore. Jerry came in, and we stood at the kitchen window. "Why won't she give up? Lay her head down and stop that ridiculous smiling," I said. "What in the world does she have to smile about?"

We were running out of time. I phoned the vet and told him we were bringing Mollie in. I drove, and Jerry got in the backseat, holding Mollie. She laid her head back on his shoulder like a child, and I wondered if Jerry might be remembering the first time he brought her home on Christmas Eve.

Looking at passing cars as I drove, I saw that none of them contained dogs. Suddenly I envied people who didn't allow themselves to love a dog in such a ridiculous fashion. Why were we dog people anyway? Why couldn't we love rocks or butterflies?

In a few moments we were in the familiar examination room. Mollie was on the sterile, steel table, which she didn't like. The vet came in and said, "Hey, Mollie." He examined her and then in a direct manner for which I will always be grateful, he said, "She has absolutely no control over her bladder or bowels. They are totally destroyed. If we operate, you will have to give her an enema daily and she will have chronic kidney infections and endless pain. She will require constant attention. You really have no choice."

I heard myself say, "No!"

The vet said quietly to Jerry, "You will need to sign some papers."

I heard my husband say, "Of course." I was grateful for his courage and quick action. They left the room, and Mollie and I were alone, my hand on her. She was half sitting up, looking directly into my eyes. All my emotions seemed frozen. I knew they would thaw out at home, but I was grateful that for now I stood like a mannequin. No feelings. No movement. No thoughts. No words. When the vet came back in the room, I moved toward the door to leave. *Don't look back*, I told myself. *Don't you dare look back.*

I looked back. Mollie and I stared at each other. I knew she wanted to wag her tail because that impossible smile crossed her face. Not understanding how it was possible, I walked mechanically out of the room.

At home, Jerry and I still had Mollie's fur clinging to us. We brushed ourselves off. The clothes didn't matter. It was our hearts and spirits that needed help.

Jerry changed into office clothes, kissed me and left for work. I didn't manage my usual "Have a good day." In my heart I just wanted him to get through it. The children were off playing; our daughter at work. They had taken it much better than Jerry or I. I was almost angry with them for being able to handle it, when I couldn't.

I was alone, standing at the kitchen window, wanting to look out into the backyard, but afraid to. *This is ridiculous. I can't be afraid of my own backyard. I have to live here.* But I knew I was afraid. I couldn't make myself walk out into a yard without Mollie. I flung myself on the sofa in the den and stared at the ceiling. My emotions were alive again. I cried out, calling Mollie's name over and over. *I'm some kind of a nut*, I thought as I sobbed. I couldn't get myself together. I had to have some kind of relief. The grief that held me in a vise seemed to be cutting off my breath, as though I were being held under water.

Then I remembered in Psalms (34:18) it said that the Lord is close to the brokenhearted. "God," I called out, as though He were up in the kitchen, "please come to me. It doesn't matter that it's just a dog. My heart is broken. You promised to be close to me. You promised! Please come and start a healing process in me. I need You."

Almost instantly my grief shifted into another gear. A lower one. I felt it. I wasn't panicky anymore. My crying stopped as if a dam had been shut down by the engineer. I got up off the sofa and brushed my hair back out of my face. I walked toward the door. I stepped outside. "Thank You, God."

The yard was still and quiet and very, very empty. I walked over to Mollie's house and shut the door. I picked up her dish, ball and old sock and took them to the shed. I emptied the water out of the wheelbarrow and put it away.

It was a strange experience walking through the yard alone. Mollie had always escorted me . . . to the garden, clothesline, birdbath . . . wherever. But now I walked slowly and victoriously over every inch of the yard. I felt as if I had been helped to win a great battle. Healing surely had begun in my broken heart.

Of course I still miss Mollie, but I am now able to recall the four years of happiness and intense love she brought to us. And I will always hold fast to the tremendous truth that I learned through losing her. God longs to be close to the brokenhearted. But He waits for us to cry out to Him. Then, regardless of what caused the pain, He responds to our deepest, our most desperate needs.

Petti Goes Home at 19

Somebody's lying
In my still backyard,
And she won't get up—

A pup who chewed
The bathroom rug,
Then scattered bits
Of yarn like snowflakes.

A sleek black temptress
Who pawed and purred,
And after the last
Mashed jelly bean,
Rubbed her fur-embroidered
Nose
Into my palm.

Nursemaid the night
David broke his arm,
Sitting on his stomach,
Keeping harm away.

Exuberant actress
In Julie's plays,
Simon Legree or
Sister Petite,
Lassie or Silver
Or a stalk of wheat.

Latterly, a lady most
Elderly,
Using four canes—
Gravely saluting
Both collars and chains.
Sightless and soundless,
Blameless, beloved.

Cushion,
Counsel,
Comrade,
Courier—

God, how can my happening
Happen without her?

Somebody's lying
In my still backyard,
And I can't even go close
Her eyes.

I'm crying too hard.

— *Sallie Chesham*

Canine Coming!

God, I want insistently to question
Whether
Among the marvelous, mystical,
Majestic mansions
Which You have prepared
For the holy whosoever,
There is an assortment
Of dog dorms, cottages
And condominiums,
Well stocked with old bones.

Because today there's
A little black and white
Dog named Petti
Coming Your way,
And You'd better be ready
For her.

Or don't count on me
Keeping You company
There—

Some other day.

— *Sallie Chesham*

A CORNER, PLEASE, FOR ONE SMALL LIFE

Margaret E. Sangster

It was a cold blustering night, and when I opened the door, in stepped the major, his coat dusted with snow. He kissed me and said, "I'm leaving right away, Aunt Margaret—have to be back at West Point by dawn."

"Can't I even give you a bite to eat?" I began, but he shook his head.

"No can do," he told me, "but there's something else you can do." He hesitated. "When I went past the library this morning, he was sitting in the deep snow. And when I started home for lunch, he was still sitting in the snow, so I picked him up. But we can't keep him at our house because of Butch." Butch was half Airedale and half coyote. "He isn't pretty, Aunt Margaret, but he has personality-plus!" He reached into his pocket and produced the very thinnest black-and-white kitten I'd ever seen. "You'll love him before the week's out!"

"You know I have two Persians and an Afghan already," I protested weakly, but the major's hand was resting on the doorknob.

"Your Persians will welcome a kitten," he said. "And the Afghan's used to cats. Be seeing you, Aunt Margaret!" He quickly left, and I stood with the trembling black-and-white kitten in my hands.

"What am I going to do with you?" I asked aloud. "I don't need you—I don't want you. You're homely!"

But before the week was out, the major's prophecy had come true. I *did* love the black-and-white kitten—maybe because he needed me. I named him Major, of course, for his West Point godfather.

I learned immediately that Major was indeed a personality kitten. In a matter of split seconds he made friends with my Persians and the Afghan hound and he peered at me with an adoration I didn't deserve. He was unusual in other ways too.

One icy day a half-frozen bird fell into the largest drift in my garden, and Major lifted it in his mouth, gently, and carried it to me—he remembered what it was like to be half-frozen. He stood beside me, purring, as I fed the bird from a medicine dropper, and soon the bird recovered and went on its way rejoicing.

Major became the protector of all small wildlife in the area. I can't tell you how many chipmunks and squirrels he rescued from certain death at the paws of my Persians.

Time went on. We moved from a large house to a small one, then to an ancient farmhouse in the Berkshire Hills. But Major didn't object to a change of scene—home to him was any place in which I lived. I noticed, however, that he seemed to tire easily—he'd got off to a bad start physically.

One afternoon I went to the village market and as I came back into the house and dropped my bag of groceries on a stand in the hall, Major didn't come trotting to meet me as he usually did. I found him sleeping quietly in his favorite chair—too quietly. As tears ran down my cheeks, I knew something precious had gone out of my life.

How can I explain what this cat meant to me? Maybe, in some sense, I was allowed to be God's agent with this small life to teach me something. Major looked to me for comfort and love and assurance—as I have learned to look to God.

As I glance back across the years, I realize that at times I fell short of Major's faith and abused his trust. There was a blazing day in mid-summer when his water dish remained empty. There was a long night when he was unwittingly imprisoned in a storage closet. But I am sure his devotion for me never changed, despite my carelessness.

Major was only a cat—and a cat's life is both short and trivial in a world where so many humans know hunger and grief. But even so, that life contributed happiness. And so I am wondering if it might be possible for the Almighty to find a small place for him in Heaven. Perhaps there is some unclaimed corner, cozy and forgotten, where a kitten can purr a rhythmic response to the angels' song.

All God's Creatures was created by the book department of the company that publish *Guideposts*, a monthly magazine filled with true stories of people's adventures in faith. If you have enjoyed this book, we think you'll find help and inspiration in the exciting stories that appear in our magazine. *Guideposts* is not sold on the newsstand. It's available by subscription only. And subscribing is easy. All you have to do is write.

Guideposts Associates, Inc.
39 Seminary Hill Road
Carmel, New York, 10512.

For those with special reading needs, *Guideposts* is published in Big Print, Braille, and Talking Magazine.

At the same time, you might be interested in ordering the current volume of *Daily Guideposts*, an annual volume of daily devotionals. Many of the stories in *All God's Creatures* appeared first in past volumes of *Daily Guideposts*.